Albert Garnier

Scientific Billiards

Garnier's Practice Shots, with hints to Amateurs

Albert Garnier

Scientific Billiards
Garnier's Practice Shots, with hints to Amateurs

ISBN/EAN: 9783743419629

Manufactured in Europe, USA, Canada, Australia, Japa

Cover: Foto ©Andreas Hilbeck / pixelio.de

Manufactured and distributed by brebook publishing software (www.brebook.com)

Albert Garnier

Scientific Billiards

SCIENTIFIC BILLIARDS.

GARNIER'S PRACTICE SHOTS,

WITH HINTS TO AMATEURS.

BY
ALBERT GARNIER.

NEW YORK
D. APPLETON & COMPANY, 1, 3, & 5 BOND STREET.
1880.

COPYRIGHT BY
D. APPLETON AND COMPANY,
1880.

PREFACE.

WITHIN the last few years, the game of billiards has become so much improved and has undergone such important modifications in its theory and practice that its character is now entirely changed. It has long been recognized as a most healthful and entertaining form of recreation. A player, even of moderate skill, finds in it complete mental relaxation and an amount of general muscular exercise which can not fail to be beneficial, especially to persons of sedentary life. In an ordinary game of one hundred points, each player must walk a half a mile or more, and the muscles of the upper part of the body, especially of the arms, are constantly brought into play. For those who are harassed by the cares of business or of professional work, the game of billiards affords amusement combined with moderate physical exercise, both of which are too often neglected; while men of leisure will find its study and practice an inexhaustible source of pleasurable excitement and interest.

PREFACE.

The American game, as it was played a quarter of a century ago, seemed, at the time, to be scarcely susceptible of much improvement in its general principles. Old players can well remember the six-by-twelve tables with six pockets and four balls, the "running the spot-ball," the combination-shots of pockets and carroms, etc., when a run of a hundred points was considered marvelous. As professional players became more skillful, the game was made more and more difficult. First, "running the spot" was barred; then the tables were made with but four pockets; then tables were made without pockets and the "push-shot" was barred; experts soon became able to make immense runs in a corner of the table, and "nursing the balls" in the corner was restricted; later the standard table was reduced in size to five by ten feet, and three balls were used instead of four; the so-called rail-play then came into vogue, and players began to make runs of hundreds; and finally, in the last grand tournament held in this city, playing on the "rail" was restricted. Amateurs, however, seldom possess the dexterity and "nerve" to make long runs on the rail; and the rules adopted by a committee of experts in 1873, which are given in an Appendix, are sufficiently rigid for ordinary players.

The great superiority of the three-ball billiards must be sufficiently evident to all who have studied and practiced the modern game. The fundamental principle in billiards is to make each shot with certainty and accuracy, but to play in such a way as to leave the balls, after making a count, in a favorable position. A fourth ball

PREFACE

on the table brings a disturbing element into the game; and a good player, even, with four balls, falls into the habit of playing too much for single shots. In the three-ball game, there are certain standard shots, constantly occurring in practice, which can either be played correctly, so as to gather the balls for a run, or they can be made, but in such a way as to leave the balls in difficult positions. The diagrams in the body of this book illustrate the proper way of playing such shots. An attempt has been made to render these diagrams practical and to put the science of the game within the reach of those who play simply for recreation and amusement. Any amateur who will study and practice these shots will certainly very soon feel a new interest in the game. It is for amateurs that this book has been written; and few if any "fancy-shots" have been introduced. I have made the science of billiards the study of my life, and, while I naturally have nothing to say of the actual strength of my game, my long experience as a professional player and as a teacher has given me a fair knowledge of what an amateur player can easily learn. Rail-playing and the *massé* shots, which latter were first satisfactorily illustrated in this country by the celebrated player, Berger, can hardly be learned without the aid of a teacher; but I venture to say that the general principles of scientific billiards can be readily acquired by a player of ordinary skill if he will faithfully study and practice the shots according to my diagrams.

In the hope of increasing the growing popular interest in billiards, and of aiding those who are desirous of improving themselves in the game, this book is presented, with some diffidence, to the public, that have always treated me with considerate kindness. The work is respectfully dedicated to American amateurs and to my pupils.

ALBERT GARNIER.

NEW YORK, 918 BROADWAY, *December 1, 1879.*

INTRODUCTION.

THE standard American billiard-table is from thirty-four to thirty-five inches high, five feet wide, and ten feet in length, measured from the outer edge of the cushions. The balls are two inches and three-eighths in diameter. Most experts play with the so-called French cues, which are from fifty-five to fifty-six inches long, and weigh from fourteen to twenty-one ounces. The weight of the cue is a question of taste and habit. The proper weight for most amateurs is from seventeen to twenty ounces. The rules governing the three-ball game are given in an Appendix following the diagrams. It would be unprofitable to attempt to give minute and definite directions with regard to the manner of holding the cue and of making the "rest" or bridge with the left hand; indeed, this little book is intended for the use of those who have already mastered the rudiments of the game of billiards. It is sufficient to state, in general terms, that the cue should be held lightly with the right hand, and the "bridge" made with the left hand should always be perfectly firm and immovable, and not more than six or seven inches from the cue-ball, measuring from the ends of the fingers. The stroke should usually be made with the forearm alone, with no movement of the arm from the shoulder. Three or four preparatory movements are made with the cue before the stroke, in order to take aim; and when this has been done, the stroke should be delivered without hesitation. Many amateurs pause for a moment after taking aim, before making the stroke. This should never be done; and the stroke should be made always without a pause.

A correct judgment with regard to the proper force of every stroke can be acquired only by long practice; but the different ways in which the cue-ball should be struck in order to produce the proper effects can be easily described. The number of different kinds of stroke is not great.

The Natural Stroke.—In what may be called the natural stroke, the cue-ball is struck above the center and neither to one side nor the other. The stroke is made deliberately, that is, neither "sharply" nor too slowly. With this stroke, there is neither a "draw," an "effect" to one side or the other, nor what is called a "follow" effect; but the cue-ball gets its direction simply from the point at which it goes off from the first object-ball. This stroke is used in making a simple carrom or a carrom with one or more cushions when no side-effect is desired. The side-effect is used when it is desired to make the cue-ball deviate from its natural direction after it has struck a cushion.

Side-Effect.—This term is synonymous with "English" or "twist." It may be used with or without the "draw" or the "follow." The simple side-effect is produced by striking the ball above the center and on one side or the other of its vertical diameter. In this stroke, the ball is not only propelled forward by the cue, but it receives a twist, or a rotary motion around its vertical axis. This rotary motion may be regulated by the manner of striking the cue-ball. When it is desired to make this as strong as possible, the cue-ball is struck very much to one side or the other, and the stroke is quick and sharp. It requires considerable judgment and practice to learn to put the exact twist on the cue-ball necessary to make the shots as they occur in a game.

Reverse Side-Effect.—In making a shot with the "reverse-twist," the cue-ball is struck on the side opposite to the direction which the ball is to take after it has gone off from the first object-ball. It must be remembered, however, that the reverse-effect "slows" the cue-ball, particularly after the cue-ball has struck a cushion. When the side-effect has the same direction as that of the cue-ball, the ball runs faster after it has struck a cushion than if the natural stroke had been used.

There are certain shots in which the side-effect is opposite to the direction taken by the cue-ball after it has left the first object-ball and before it has struck a cushion, but still having the same direction as the cue-ball after it has struck the cushion. In such shots, the velocity of the cue-ball increases after it has struck the first cushion. An example of this is in diagram No. 12.

When a side-effect is given to the cue-ball, and the ball passes directly across the table from one side-cushion to the other, the direction given to the ball by the twist is reversed when it strikes the second cushion. An example of this is in diagram No. 20.

The Follow-Stroke.—The follow-stroke is played somewhat differently in different positions of the balls. When the three balls are two or three feet apart and it is desired to follow from one to the other, the cue-ball is struck above the center with a slow stroke, letting the cue follow the cue-ball rather slowly after the stroke has been made.

When the cue-ball is very near the first object-ball and the second object-ball is four or five feet distant, the stroke is quicker and sharper, and the cue-ball is struck more on top.

When the first object-ball is five or six feet from the cue-ball, and the second object-

INTRODUCTION.

ball is quite near the first, the cue-ball is struck considerably below the center, with a slow stroke. An example of this is in diagram No. 42.

The follow-stroke with side-effect is used when the cue-ball strikes a cushion before it strikes the second object-ball.

The Half-Follow Stroke.—In many positions of the balls, a half-follow stroke in making a simple carrom will gather the balls more successfully than if the shot be made with the natural stroke. When the half-follow is played, the stroke is frequently made with a slight reverse side-effect. In the half-follow, the stroke is precisely the same as in the follow, but the cue-ball takes a different direction after it goes off from the first object-ball, this direction depending upon the point at which the first object-ball has been struck.

"Slowing" the Cue-Ball.—It is sometimes desirable to drive the first object-ball around the table and to follow slowly upon the second object-ball, as in diagram No. 39. To "slow" the cue-ball, strike it at the center with a quick, sharp stroke. With this stroke, the cue-ball takes little or no rotary motion from the cue, and it follows slowly to the second object-ball, having transmitted most of its force to the first object-ball. Shots of this kind, to be played accurately, require considerable practice.

Draw-Shots.—The draw-shots are by far the most important shots in the game. It is possible to learn to play them with absolute accuracy; and usually, if they fail to count, the balls are left in a very favorable position for the adversary. In the draw-shots, the direction is almost invariably to be taken from the first object-ball. When the cue-ball is drawn back without side-effect, if the first object-ball be hit at the proper point, the shot will be made with absolute certainty. A reverse side-effect is used only when it is desired to "slow" the cue-ball. A side-effect following the direction of the cue-ball is never used unless it be intended to make the cue-ball strike a cushion. In making the draw-shot, the cue-ball is struck low down with a quick, sharp stroke, and the cue should pass about four inches beyond the original situation of the ball. It is a very common fault with amateurs to draw the cue back after making the stroke. This should never be done in an ordinary draw-shot. When the cue-ball is very near the first object-ball, of course the cue can not follow the ball. In shots of this kind, the stroke should be as quick and sharp as possible. These shots are quite difficult. One great advantage of the draw-shot is that it very frequently "gathers" the balls. The importance of draw-shots is readily appreciated in watching a good game by professional experts, when it will be seen that they play draws more frequently than any other shots. The simple "spread" shot, like the one in diagram No. 62, is merely a modification of the draw-shot, and the direction is taken entirely from the first object-ball. In draw-and-cushion shots, like the shot in diagram No. 67, the reverse side-effect is used. In draw-and-cushion shots, like the one in diagram No. 68, the side-effect follows the direction of the cue-ball.

Massé-Shots.—Massé-shots, as given in the diagrams, are made by giving the cue-ball a strong side-effect, or a "draw" without side-effect, striking it almost vertically with the cue. These shots are often necessary in the three-ball game. Although they are not very difficult, they can hardly be learned without the aid of a teacher. They must be played with great accuracy, for if they fail to count they almost always leave the balls in a very favorable position for the adversary. Directions for making simple *massé*-shots are given under diagrams No. 94, No. 95, and No. 100.

In order to indicate approximatively the point where the first object-ball is to be struck, the following terms are used in the explanations of the diagrams: Striking the object-ball full means that the cue-ball must strike it nearly at the center; striking the object-ball one-quarter means midway between the center and the side; half-full means midway between "full" and "one-quarter"; one-third means a little more to one side than "half-full," and a little less than "one-quarter"; "fine" means more to the side than "one-quarter."

Although, in a game of billiards, the balls may be left in an almost infinite variety of positions, certain of these are shown in the diagrams which frequently occur. In such positions the shots can be played correctly, with a view of "gathering" the balls for a "run," or of leaving them in a good position for the next shot, or they can frequently be made, but in such a way as to separate the balls. The strength of a player depends upon the accuracy with which the shots are made and skill in leaving the balls in a favorable position. "Nursing" the balls and the so-called "rail-playing" are difficult and require long practice and great delicacy of touch. The art of "nursing" can not be taught by mere description. When a player has learned all the methods of striking the cue-ball and knows how to play the usual gathering-shots, he can learn to play a strong game only by practice. It must be remembered that the first object in playing a shot is to count; but, at the same time, the player should attempt always to leave the balls in a good position after the count has been made. Referring to the different kinds of stroke, their number is not great. A player has to learn only the natural stroke, the side-effect and the reverse, the follow, the half-follow, "slowing" the cue-ball, the draw and spread, and the simple *massé*-shots. Kiss-shots and cushion-first shots are shown in the diagrams and are easily learned.

NOTE.

In practicing the shots illustrated by the diagrams, players should always follow the directions printed below each diagram, and not always the exact lines of the diagrams themselves, as a few of the illustrations show slight errors in printing.

GARNIER'S PRACTICE SHOTS.

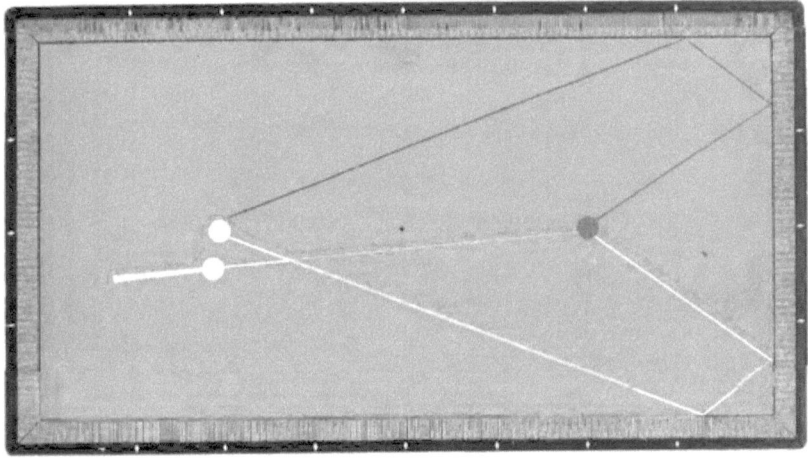

No. 1.—First Shot of the Game.

Strike your own ball on top without side-effect, the red ball half-full, and the shot will be made by two cushions, bringing the balls together.

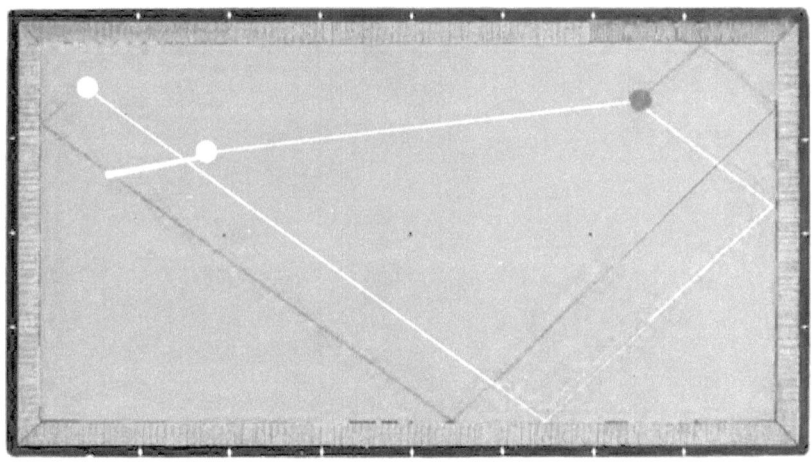

No. 2.—Round-the-Table Gathering-Shot.

Strike your own ball above the center and on the right side, the red ball one-third, and the shot will be made by two cushions, bringing the balls together.

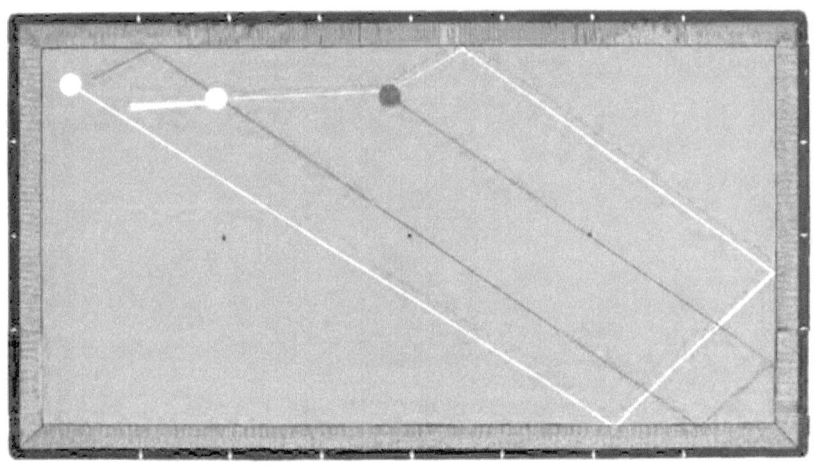

No. 3.—Round-the-Table Gathering-Shot (inside).

Strike your own ball on top and on the right side, the red ball one-third, and the shot will be made by three cushions, bringing the red with the two white balls in the left corner.

<small>Note.—In playing this shot and all shots of this kind, make the first object-ball strike the end-cushion first. You will then generally avoid the "kiss," as both balls are going in the same direction. If, however, the first object-ball should take the side-cushion first, the balls will generally "kiss," as they are going in opposite directions.</small>

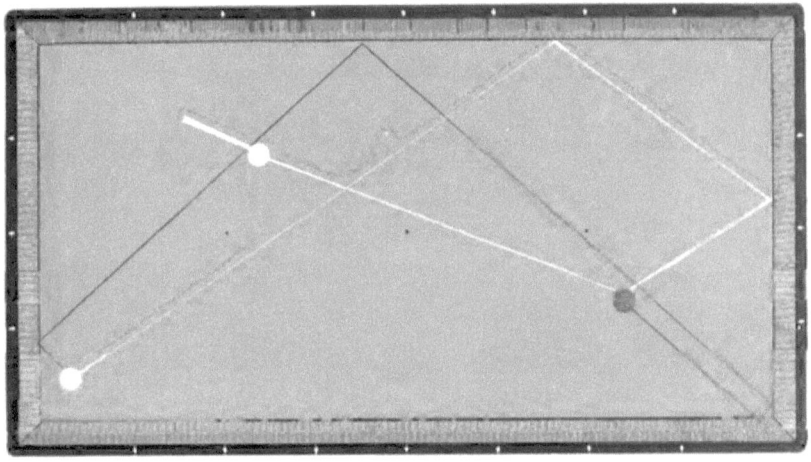

No. 4.—Round-the-Table Gathering-Shot.

Strike your own ball a little below the center and to the left, the red ball one-third, and the shot will be made by two cushions, bringing the red with the two white balls in the right corner.

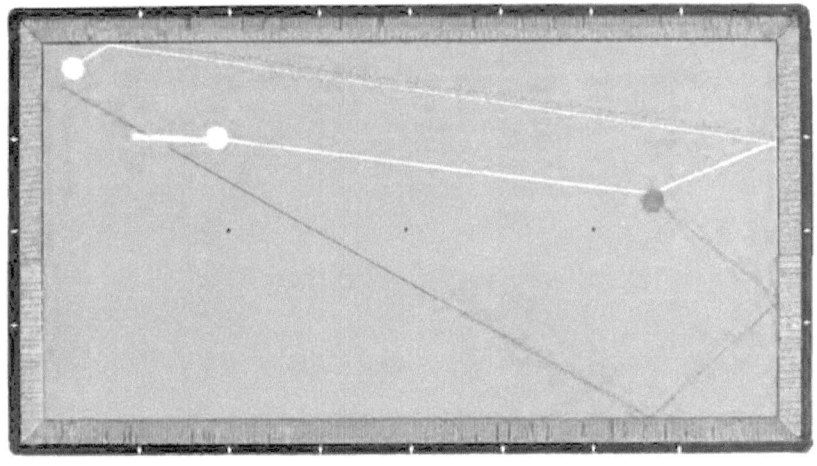

No. 5.—GATHERING-SHOT WITH REVERSE SIDE-EFFECT.

Strike your own ball a little above the center and on the right side (reverse-effect), the red ball about one-third, and the shot will be made by two cushions, bringing the balls together in the left corner.

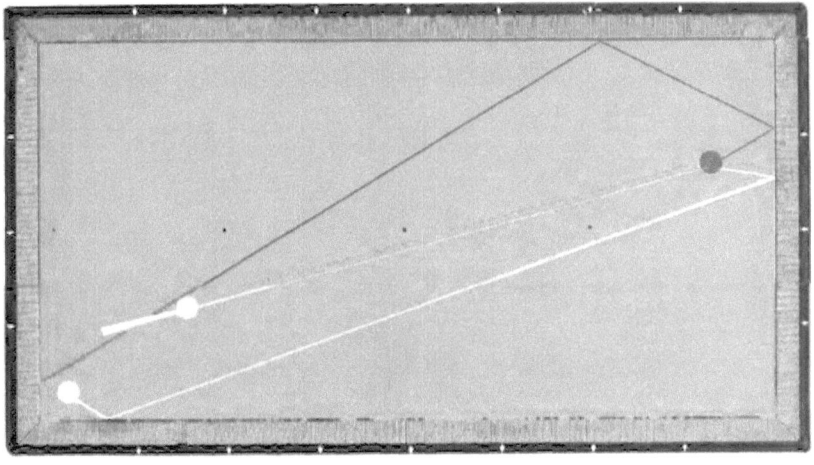

No. 6.—GATHERING-SHOT THE LENGTH OF THE TABLE.

Strike your own ball on top and without side-effect, the red ball one-third, and the shot will be made by two cushions, bringing the balls together in the right corner.

GARNIER'S PRACTICE SHOTS.

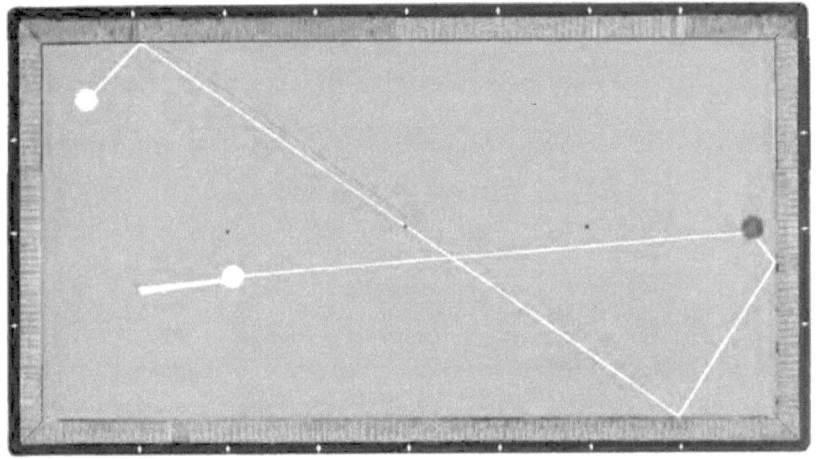

No. 7.—Round-the-Table Shot with Three Cushions.

Strike your own ball below the center, and on the right side, the red ball one-quarter, and the shot will be made by three cushions. Play the shot with rather a quick, sharp stroke.

NOTE.— The direction of the red ball is not given in the diagram as this is not a gathering-shot.

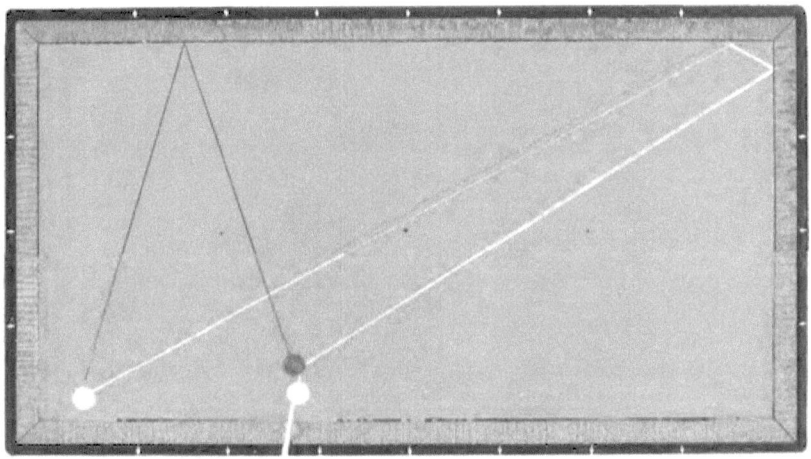

No. 8.—ROUND-THE-TABLE SHOT.

Strike your own ball a little above the center and on the left side, the red ball "fine," and the shot will be made by two cushions, bringing the red with the two white balls in the corner.

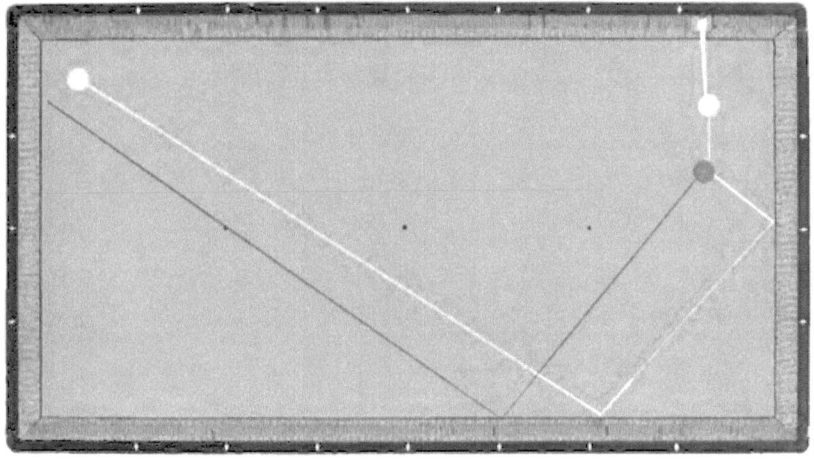

No. 9.—INSIDE ROUND-THE-TABLE SHOT.

Strike your own ball below the center and on the right side, the red ball one-quarter, and the shot will be made by two cushions, bringing the balls together in the corner. This shot should not be played too "hard."

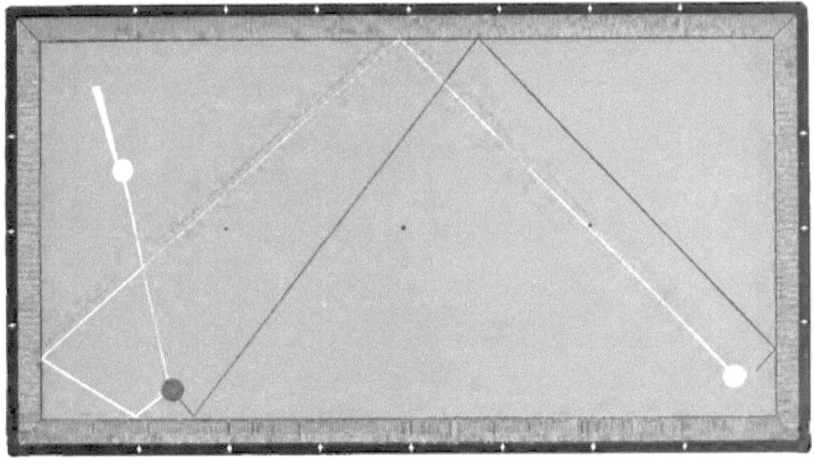

No. 10.—Round-the-Table Gathering-Shot.

Strike your own ball in the middle and on the right side, the red ball "fine," and the shot will be made by three cushions, bringing the balls together in the corner.

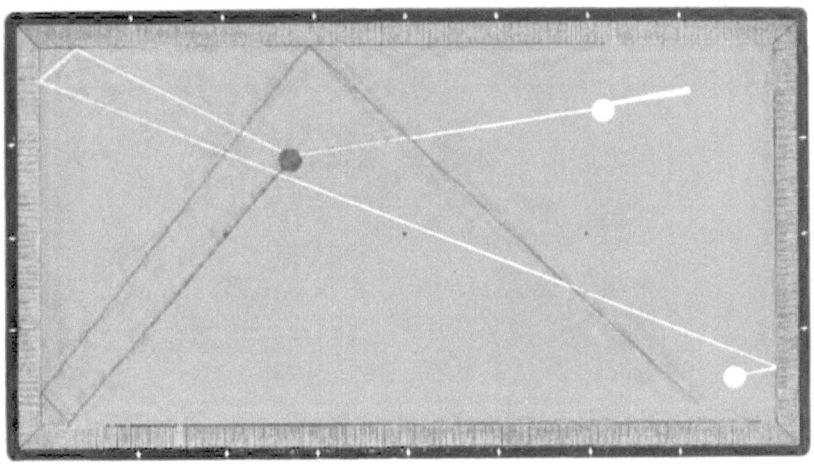

No. 11.—Shot the Length of the Table with Reverse-Effect.

Strike your own ball on top and slightly to the right, the red ball between one-third and one-quarter, and the shot will be made by two or three cushions, bringing the balls together in the corner. This shot should be played rather "hard."

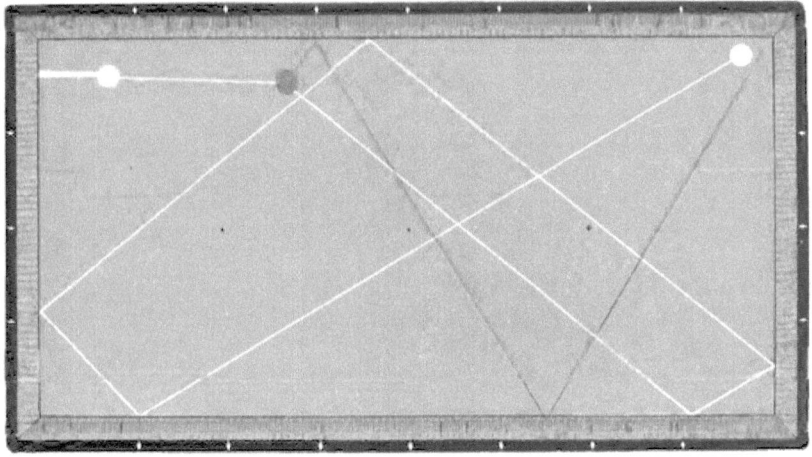

No. 12.—Twice-Round-the-Table Shot.

Strike your own ball "hard," a little below the center and on the left side, the red ball rather "fine," and the shot will be made by five cushions, bringing the balls together in the corner.

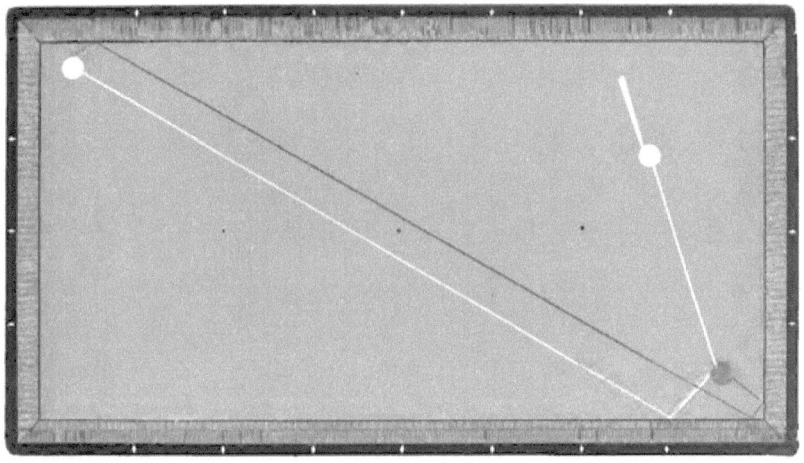

No. 13.—Gathering-Shot.

Strike your own ball in the middle and on the right side, the red ball one-quarter, and the shot will be made by one cushion. Do not play this shot too "hard," and the balls will be brought together in the corner.

GARNIER'S PRACTICE SHOTS.   14

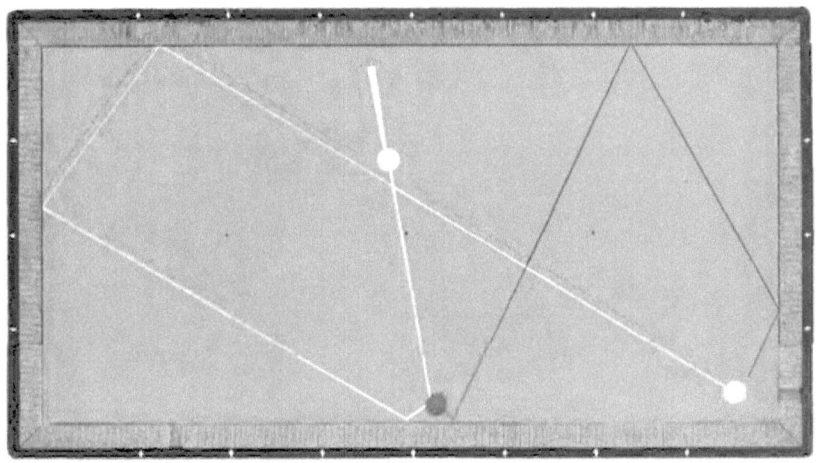

No. 14.—Round-the-Table Gathering-Shot.

Strike your own ball a little below the center and on the right side, the red ball one-quarter, and the shot will be made by three cushions, bringing the balls together in the corner.

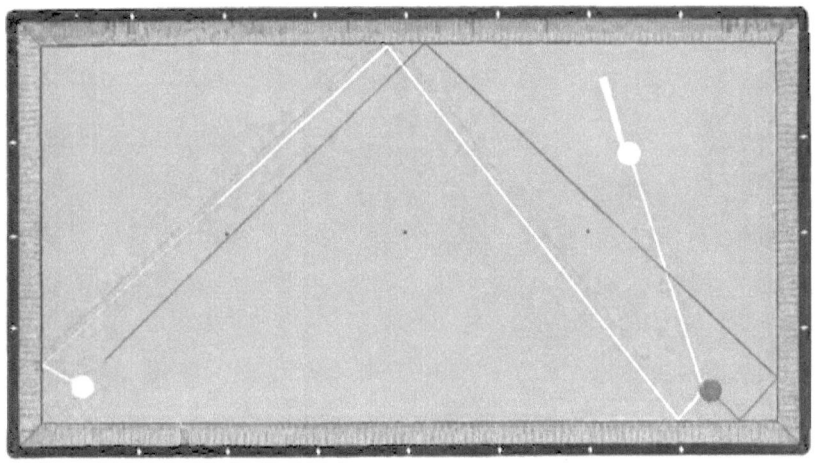

No. 15.—Twice-across-the-Table Shot.

Strike your own ball a little below the center and slightly to the right, the red ball one-quarter, and the shot will be made by two or three cushions, bringing the balls together in the corner. This shot should be played rather "hard."

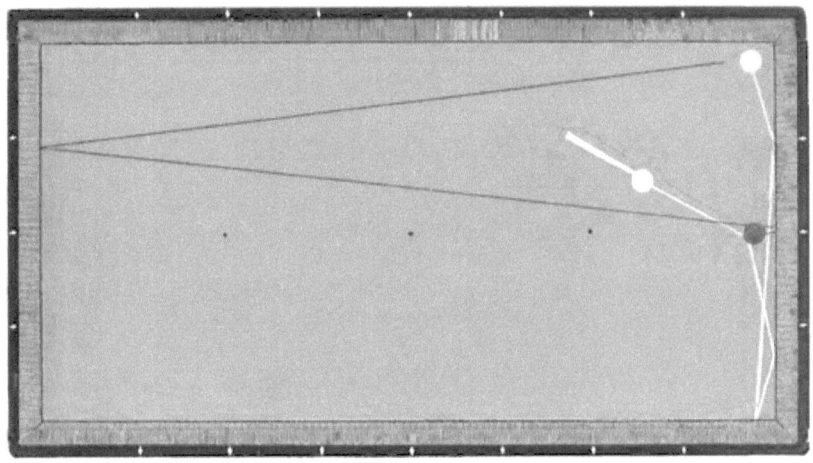

No. 16.—Across-the-Table Shot.

Strike your own ball on top and to the left, the red ball "fine," and the shot will be made by two or three cushions, bringing the balls together in the corner. This shot should be played rather "hard."

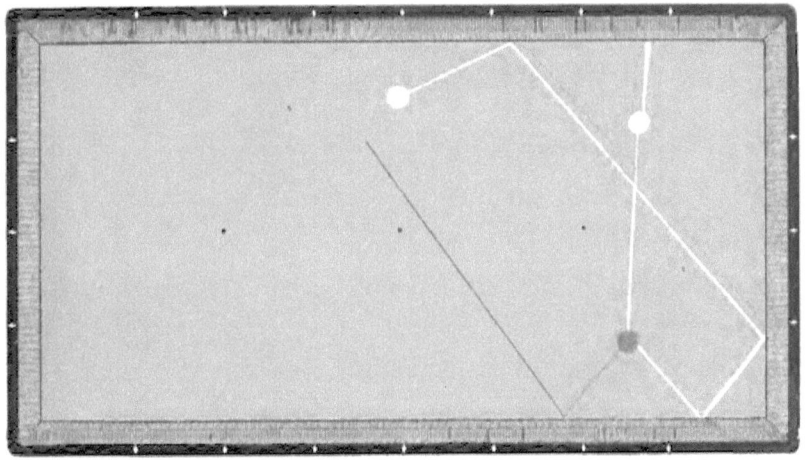

No. 17.—Across-the-Table Shot by Three Cushions.

Strike your own ball on top and to the left, the red ball one-third, and the shot will be made by three cushions, bringing the red near the other balls if the shot be not played too " hard."

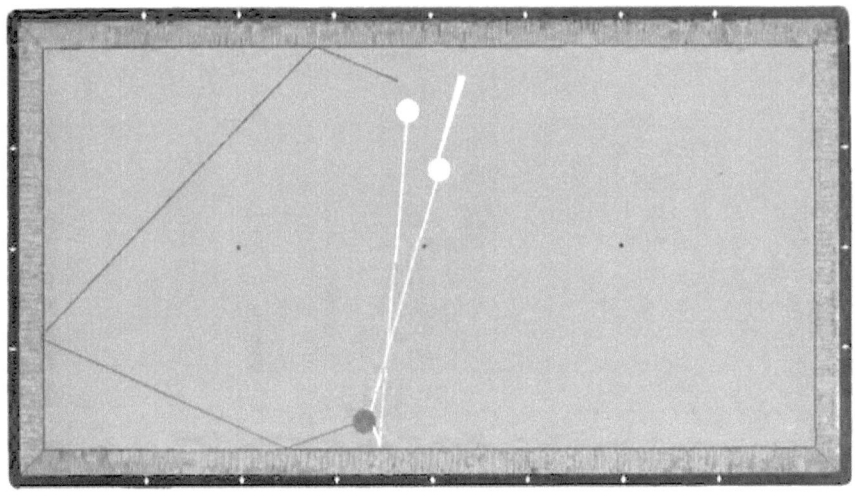

No. 18.—Across-the-Table Gathering Shot.

Strike your own ball on top and a little to the right, the red ball one-quarter, and the shot will be made by one cushion, bringing the balls together.

GARNIER'S PRACTICE SHOTS.

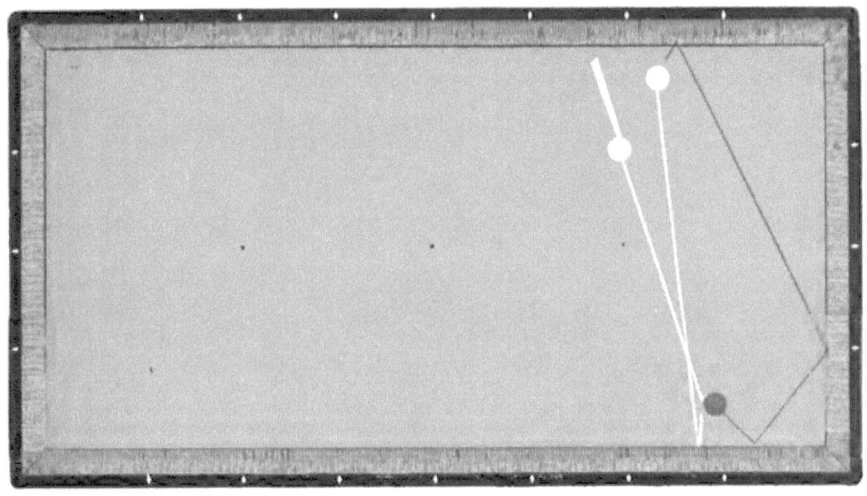

No. 19.—Across-the-Table Shot.

Strike your own ball on top, and a little to the left, the red ball one-third, and the shot will be made by one cushion, bringing the balls together. This shot should be played with the follow-stroke and not too " hard."

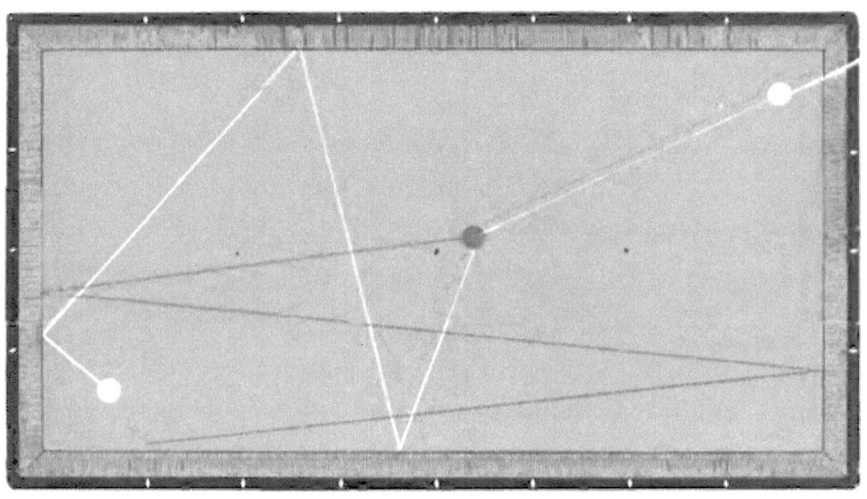

No. 20.—Twice-across-the-Table Shot.

Strike your own ball a little above the center and slightly to the left, the red ball half-full, and the shot will be made by three cushions, bringing the balls together. Play this shot "hard" and with the follow-stroke.

NOTE.—The cue-ball takes the proper side-effect after it leaves the second side-cushion.

GARNIER'S PRACTICE SHOTS.

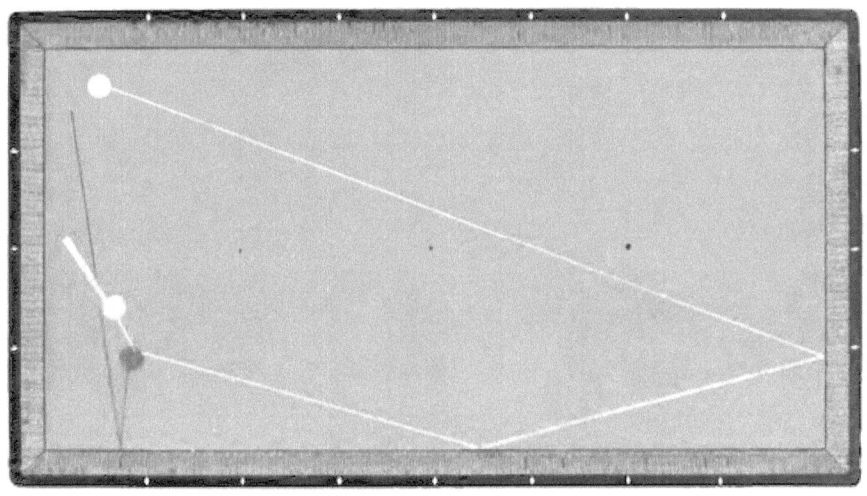

No. 21.—Gathering-Shot the Length of the Table.

Strike your own ball on top and slightly to the right, the red ball about one-third, and the shot will be made by two cushions. Play this shot rather gently, and the red ball will join the other two balls in the corner.

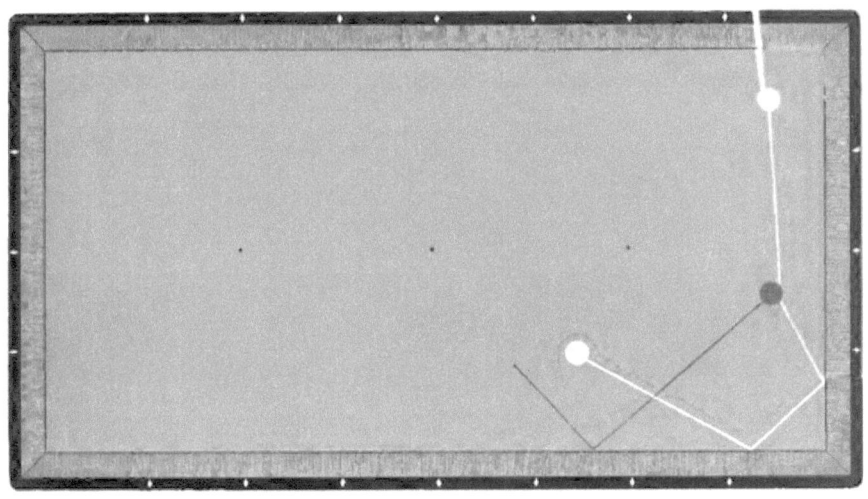

No. 22.—Gathering-Shot.

Strike your own ball a little above the center and on the right side, the red ball one-quarter, and the shot will be made by two cushions, bringing the balls together, if played gently. Hold the cue very lightly in making the stroke.

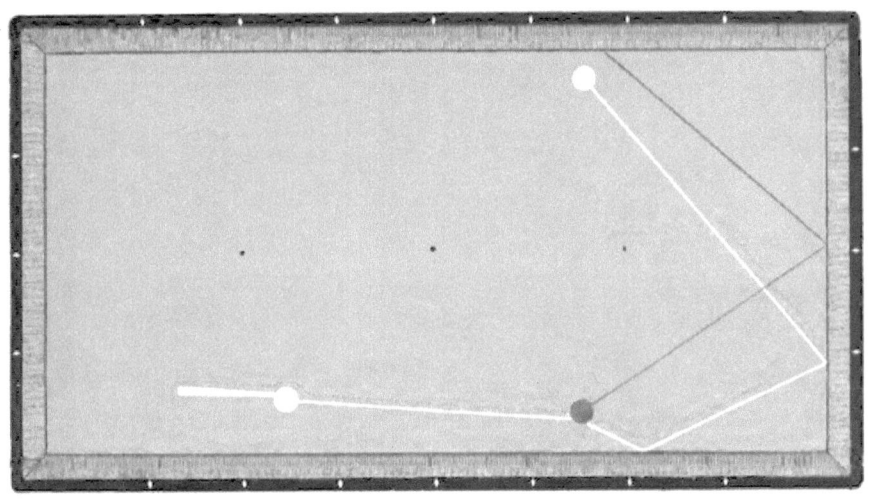

No. 23.—Gathering-Shot.

Strike your own ball on top and on the left side with the follow-stroke, the red ball one-quarter, and the shot will be made by two cushions, bringing the balls together, if played gently.

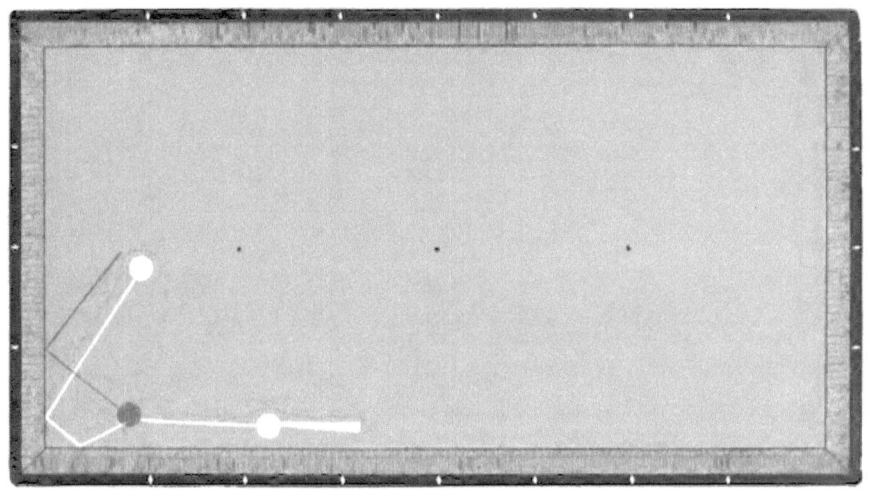

No. 24.—Gathering-Shot.

Strike your own ball on top and on the right side, the red ball about one-quarter, and the shot will be made by two cushions. This shot should be played very gently so as to leave the balls well together.

GARNIER'S PRACTICE SHOTS. 25

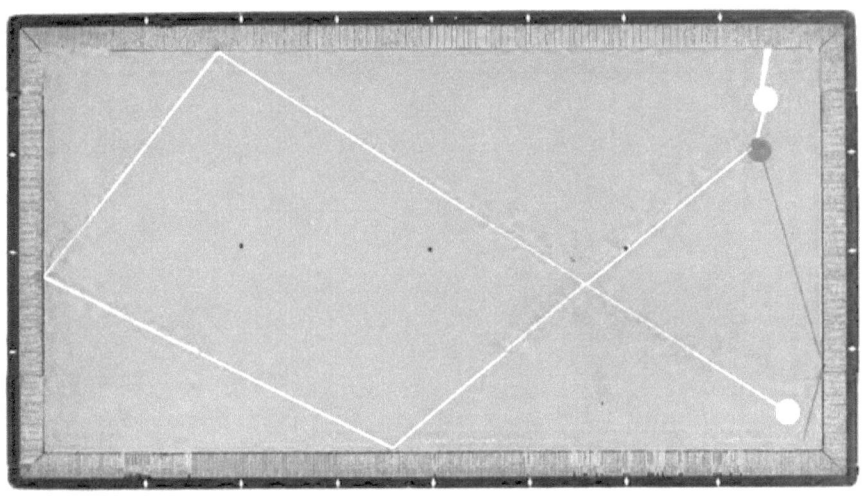

No. 25.—Round-the-Table Gathering-Shot.

Strike your own ball on top and on the right side, the red ball "fine," and the shot will be made by three cushions, leaving the balls pretty well together.

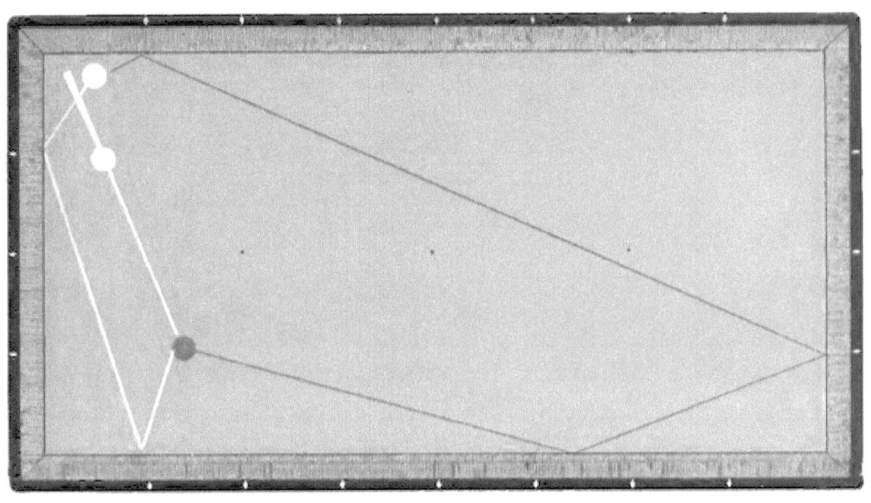

No. 26.—Across-the-Table Shot with Reverse-Effect.

Strike your own ball a little below the center and slightly to the left, the red ball one-quarter, and the shot will be made by two cushions. Play moderately "hard" in order to bring the red ball into the corner with the two white balls.

GARNIER'S PRACTICE SHOTS. 27

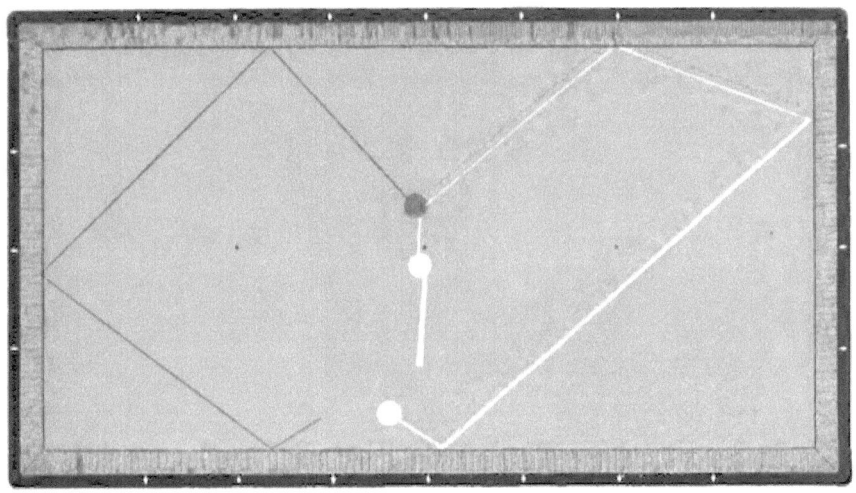

No. 27.—GATHERING-SHOT.

Strike your own ball below the center and on the right side, the red ball one-quarter, and the shot will be made by two cushions, bringing the balls together on the side-cushion. This shot should be played with moderate force.

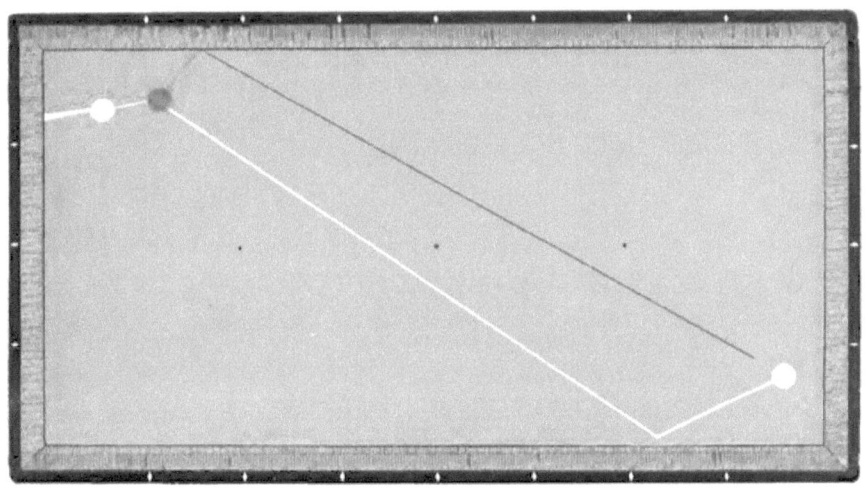

No. 28.—Half-Follow Gathering-Shot.

Strike your own ball on top and on the left side, the red ball about half-full, and the shot will be made by one cushion, the red ball joining the two white balls in the corner. This shot should be played with the follow-stroke.

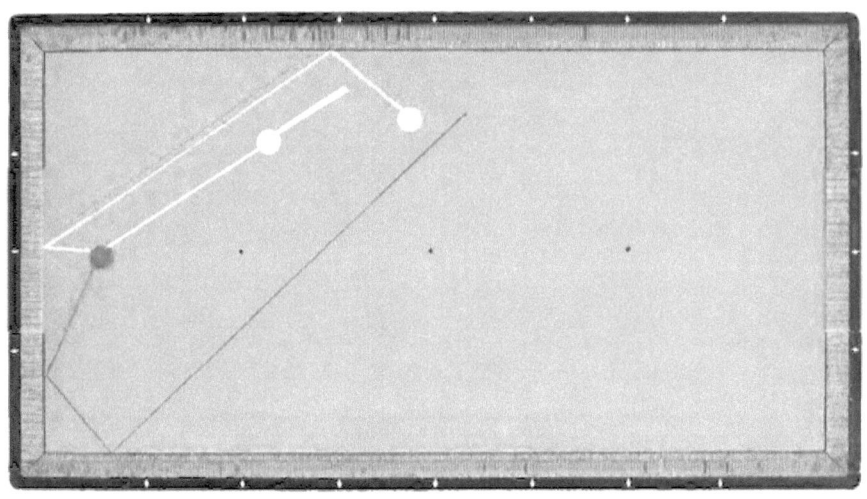

No. 29.—Gathering-Shot.

Strike your own ball a little above the center and on the right side, the red ball half-full, and the shot will be made by two cushions. This shot should be played with the follow-stroke, not too "hard," and the balls will be left pretty well together.

GARNIER'S PRACTICE SHOTS. 30

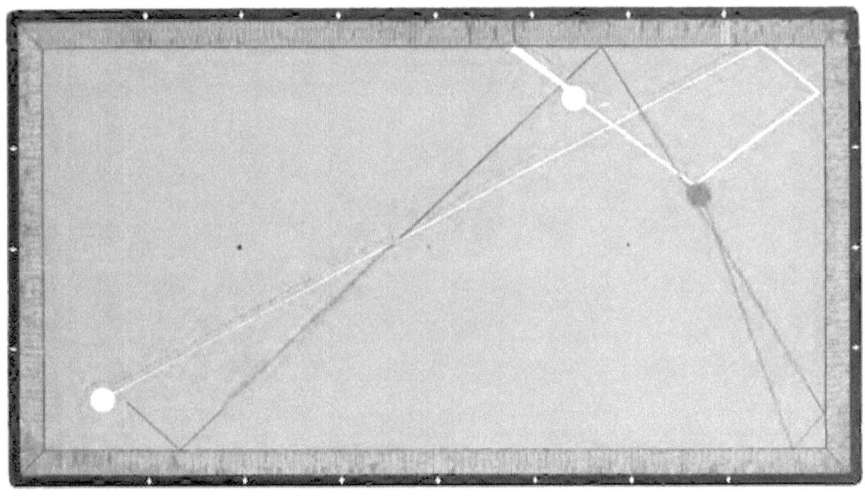

No. 30.—Round-the-Table Gathering-Shot.

Strike your own ball moderately low down and on the left side, the red ball half-full, and the shot will be made by two cushions, driving the red ball by three or four cushions to join the two white balls in the corner.

GARNIER'S PRACTICE SHOTS. 31

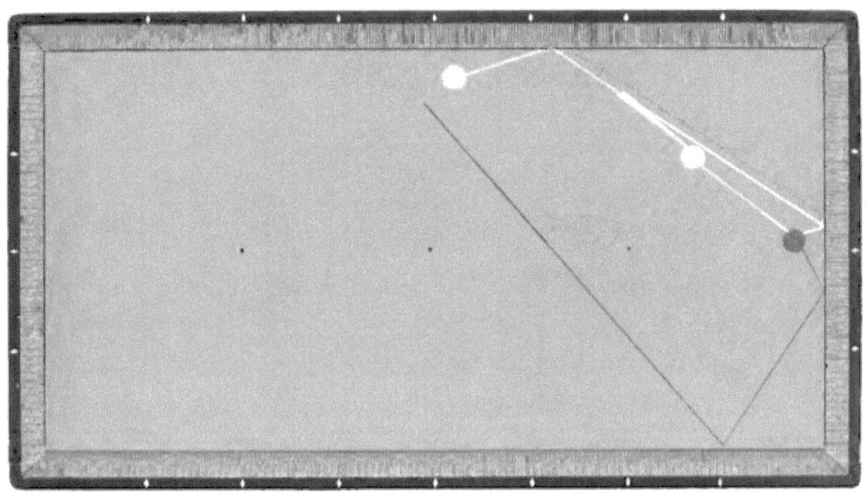

No. 31.—Gathering-Shot.

Strike your own ball a little below the center and on the left side, the red ball about half-full, and the shot will be made by two cushions. If the shot be played not too "hard," the red ball will join the two white balls near the side-cushion.

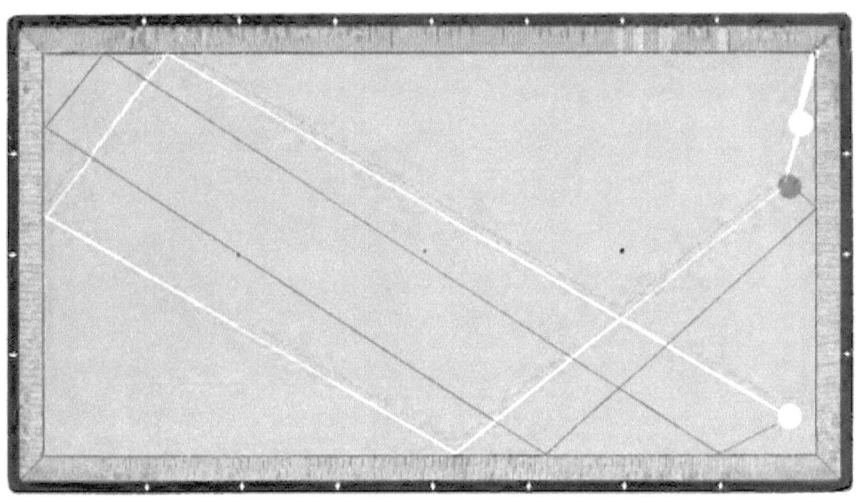

No. 32.—Round-the-Table Gathering-Shot.

Strike your own ball a little below the center and on the right side, the red ball about one-quarter, and the shot will be made by three cushions, driving the red ball around the table and into the corner. This shot should be played moderately "hard."

GARNIER'S PRACTICE SHOTS.   33

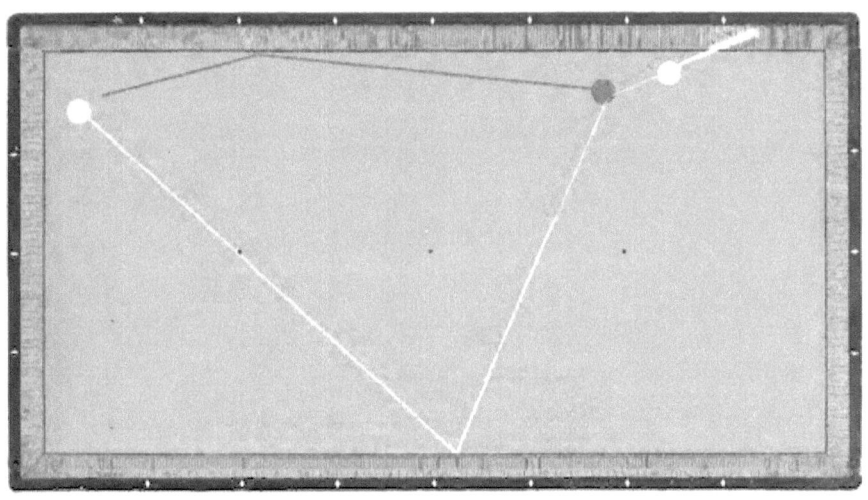

No. 33.—Gathering-Shot across the Table.

Strike your own ball on top and a little on the right side, the red ball one-quarter, and the shot will be made by one cushion, bringing the balls together in the corner.

GARNIER'S PRACTICE SHOTS. 34

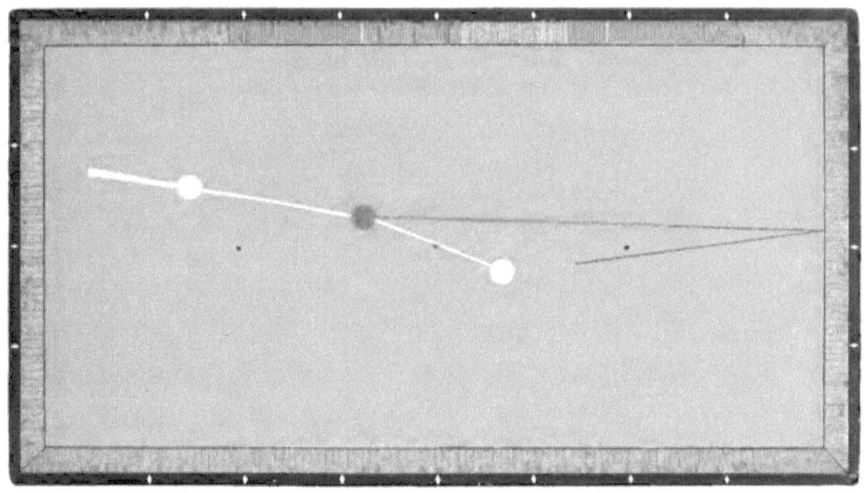

No. 34.—SIMPLE FOLLOW-SHOT.

Strike your own ball on top with no side-effect and follow directly on the second object-ball. Play this shot gently and the two balls will be left well together.

NOTE.—Hold the cue very lightly in the hand for shots of this kind.

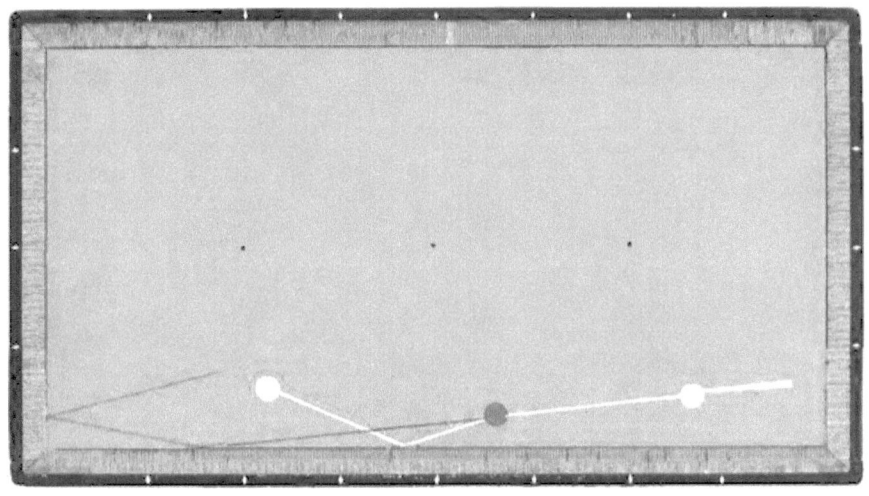

No. 35.—Follow-Shot by the Cushion.

Strike your own ball on top and a little on the right side, the red ball a little to the left, follow to the side-cushion, and then to the second object-ball. Play this shot rather gently to keep the balls together.

GARNIER'S PRACTICE SHOTS. 36

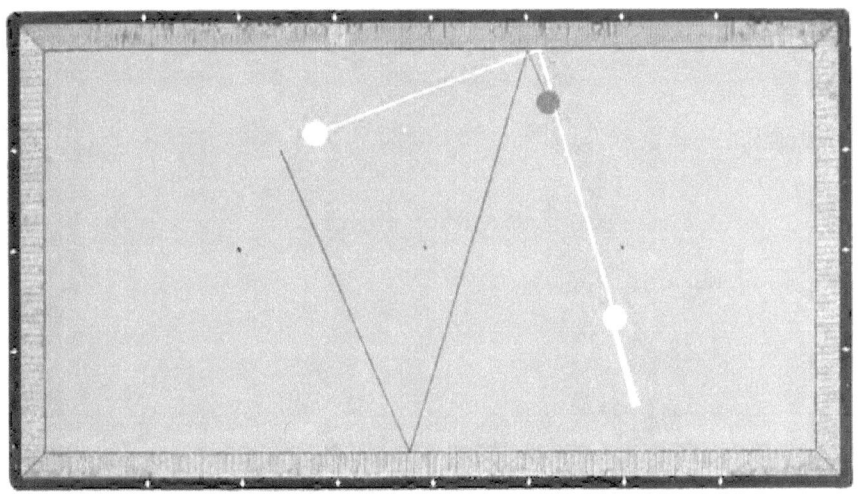

No. 36.—Follow and Cushion Shot, with Side-Effect.

Strike your own ball on top and on the left side, the red ball full, follow from the red ball to the side cushion, and the side-effect will take the cue-ball to the second object-ball. The red ball will cross the table to join the two other balls if the shot be played not too "hard."

GARNIER'S PRACTICE SHOTS. 37

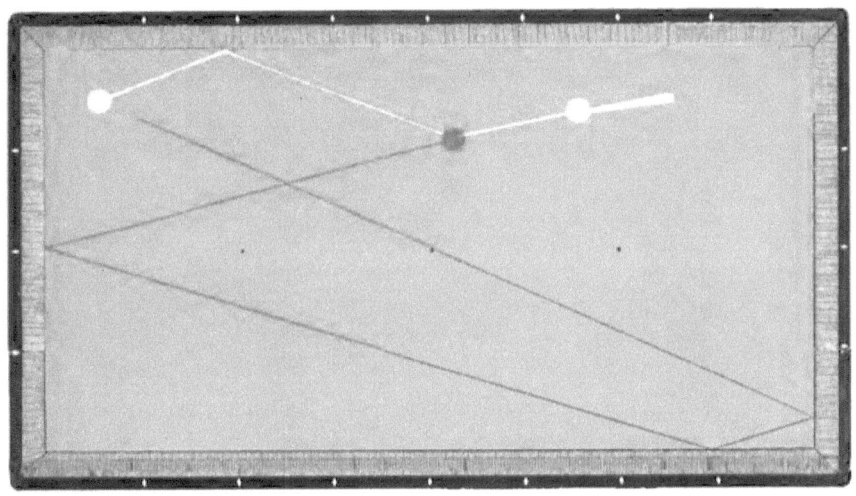

No. 37.—Gathering-Shot.

Strike your own ball a little below the center and on the left side, the red ball nearly full, "slow" your own ball and play rather "hard," and the shot will be made by one cushion, driving the red ball the length of the table and back to the corner with the other balls.

GARNIER'S PRACTICE SHOTS.

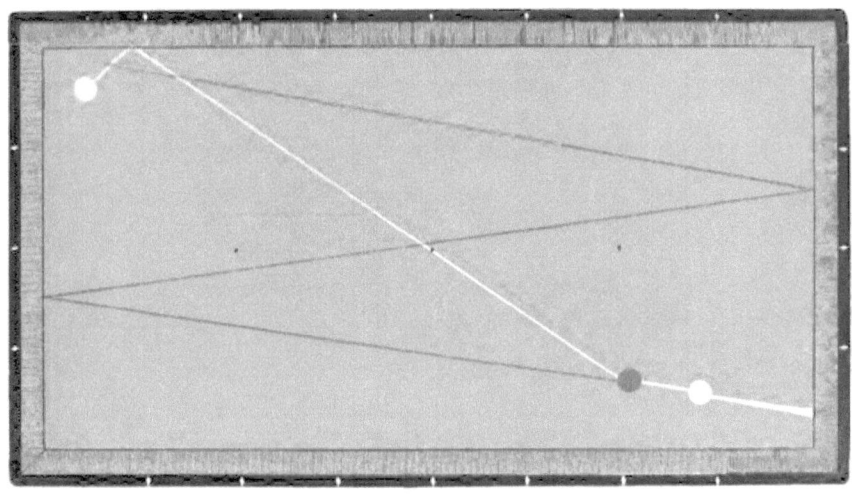

No. 38.—GATHERING FOLLOW-SHOT.

Strike your own ball rather higher than in the preceding shot and a little to the right, the red ball full, and the shot will be made by one cushion, driving the red ball the length of the table into the corner. This shot should be played rather "hard."

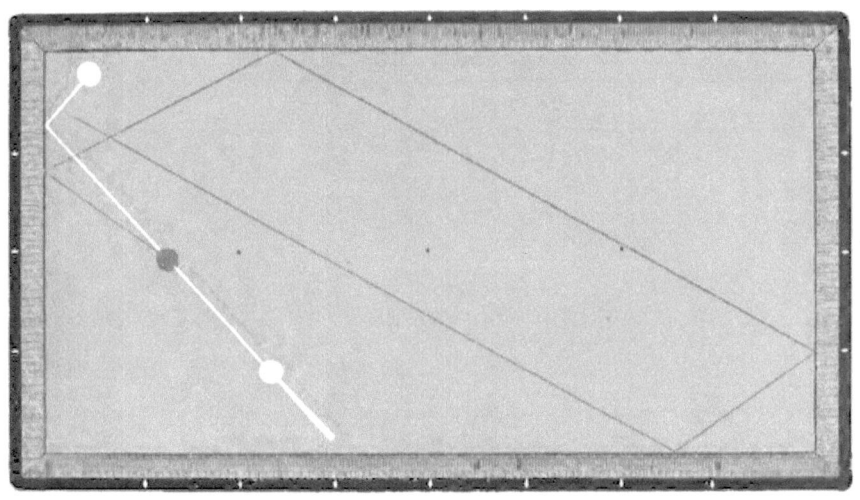

No. 39.—Follow-Shot with the Cue-Ball "slowed."

Strike your own ball "hard" and at the center with a sharp stroke, the red ball full, and follow slowly on the second object-ball, driving the red ball around the table to join the two white balls in the corner.

GARNIER'S PRACTICE SHOTS.   40

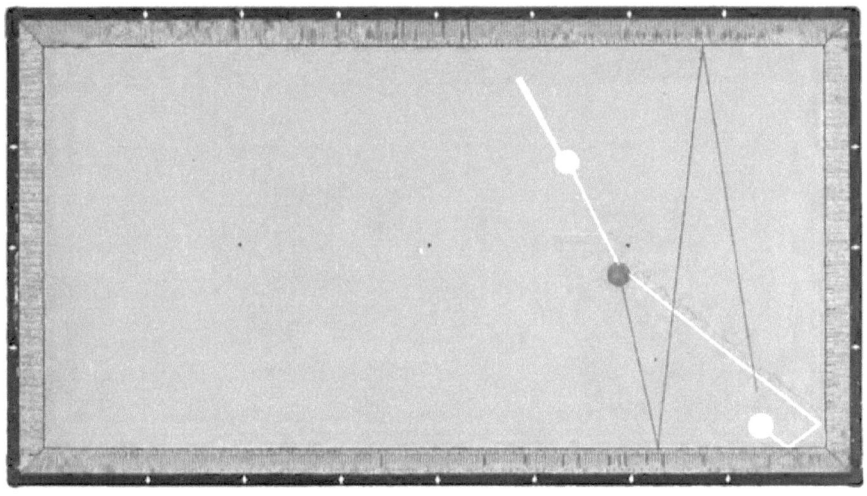

No. 40.—Gathering Half-Follow Shot.

Strike your own ball in the middle and on the right side, the red ball almost full, slowing your own ball, and the shot will be made by two cushions. Play the shot "hard," and you will cross the red ball twice and bring the balls together.

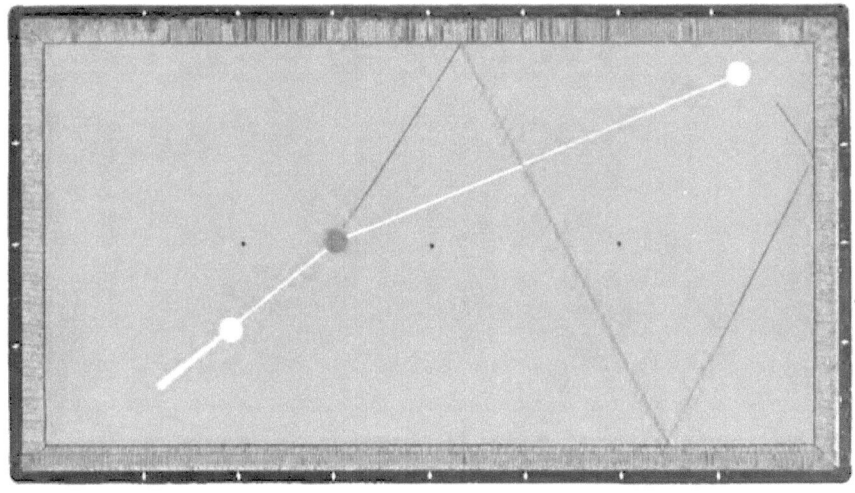

No. 41.—Gathering Follow-Shot.

Strike your own ball on top and a very little to the left, the red ball nearly full, and you will follow directly on the second object-ball, crossing the red ball into the corner.

GARNIER'S PRACTICE SHOTS. 42

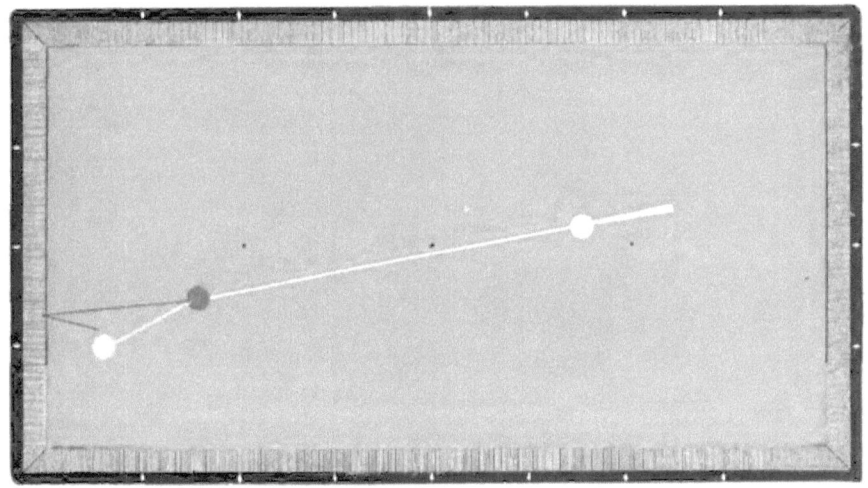

No. 42.—Follow-Shot.

Strike your own ball a little below the center and follow directly on the second object-ball. Play this shot with a slow stroke and rather gently, and the balls will be left together.

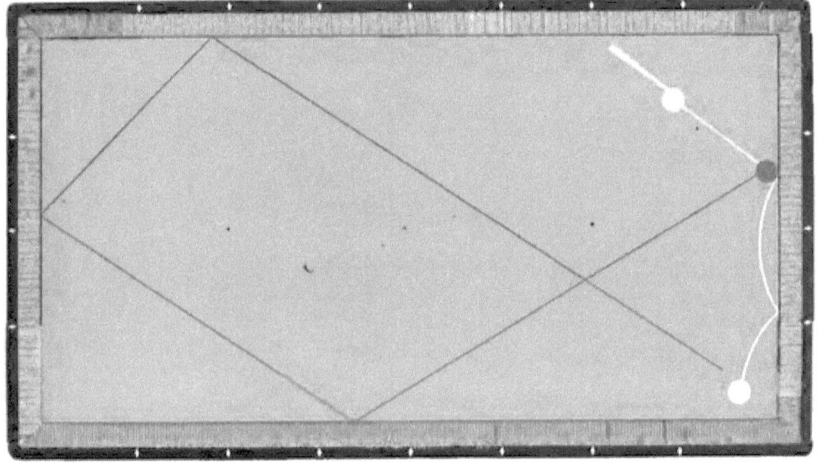

No. 43.—Follow-Shot by the Cushion.

Strike your own ball a little above the center and slightly to the left, the red ball rather full, and the count will be made by the cushion. Play the shot rather "hard" in order to drive the red ball around the table into the corner to join the two white balls.

GARNIER'S PRACTICE SHOTS. 44

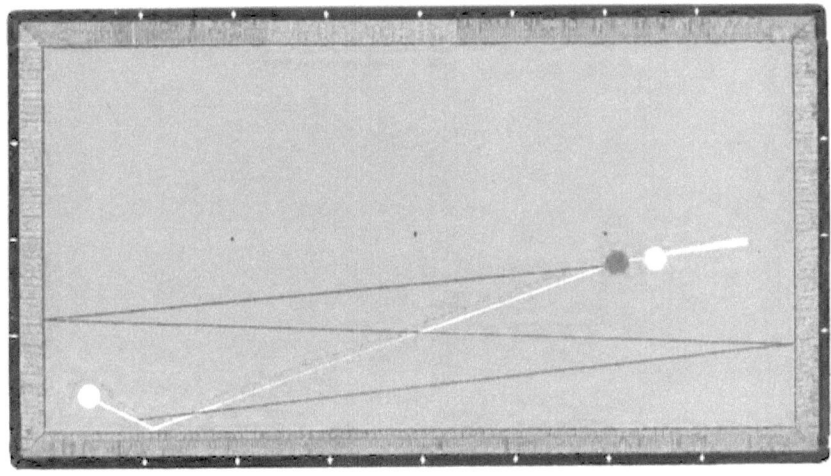

No. 44.—Follow-Shot, with the Balls near together.

When the balls are very near together, in order to avoid the "push," it is necessary to use a strong side-effect. Strike your own ball a little below the center and as much as possible to the right, and the shot will be made by one cushion, driving the red ball the length of the table into the corner to join the two white balls.

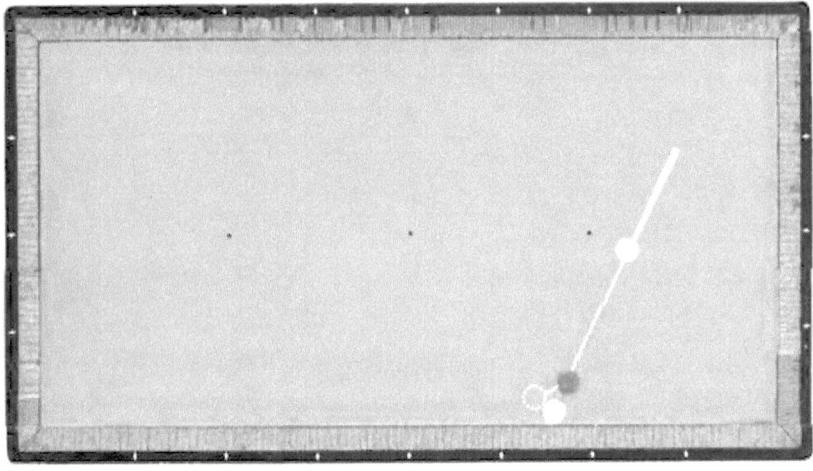

No. 45.—Follow and "Kiss Shot" with the two Object-Balls near together.

Strike your own ball on top and a little to the left, the red ball nearly full, and the cue-ball will meet the second object-ball at about the dotted circle. This is a very certain and easy shot.

GARNIER'S PRACTICE SHOTS. 46

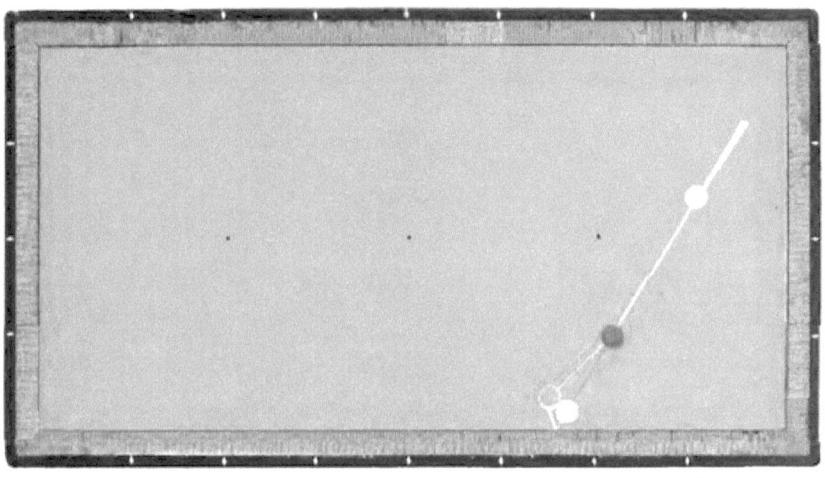

No. 46.—Follow and "Kiss-Shot.

Strike your own ball on top and a little to the left, the red ball a little fuller than in the preceding shot, and the cue-ball will meet the second object-ball at about the dotted circle. This is also an easy shot.

GARNIER'S PRACTICE SHOTS. 47

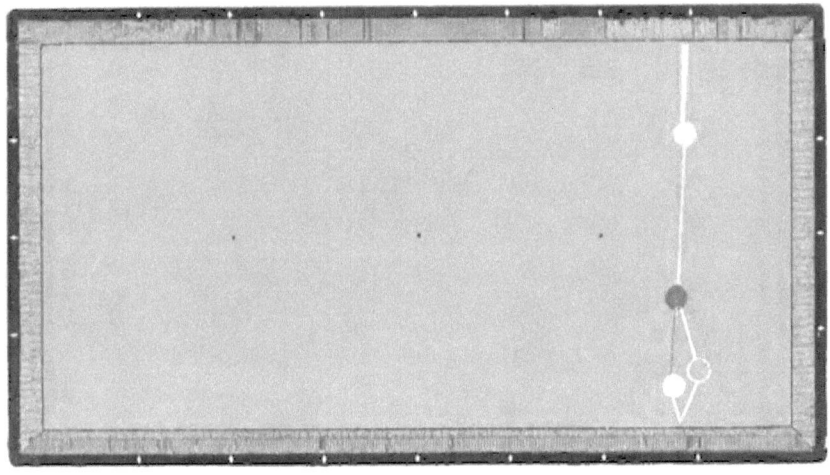

No. 47.—STRAIGHT FOLLOW AND "KISS-SHOT."

Strike your own ball on top and slightly to the right, the red ball nearly full, and the cue-ball will meet the second object-ball at about the dotted circle.

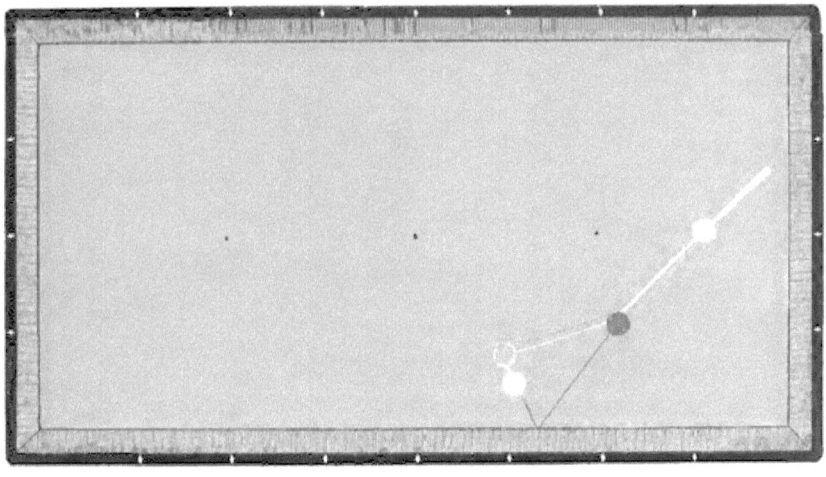

No. 48.—Follow and "Kiss-Shot."

Strike your own ball on top and slightly to the left, and play so as to make the red ball take the side-cushion and touch the second object-ball gently so that it will meet the cue-ball at about the dotted circle.

GARNIER'S PRACTICE SHOTS. 49

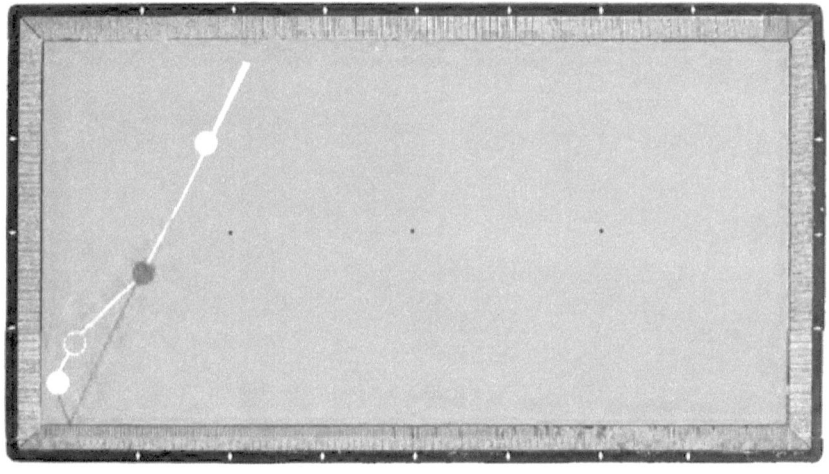

No. 49.—Follow and "Kiss-Shot."

Strike your own ball on top and a little to the left, the red ball nearly full, and the second object-ball will meet the cue-ball near the dotted circle.

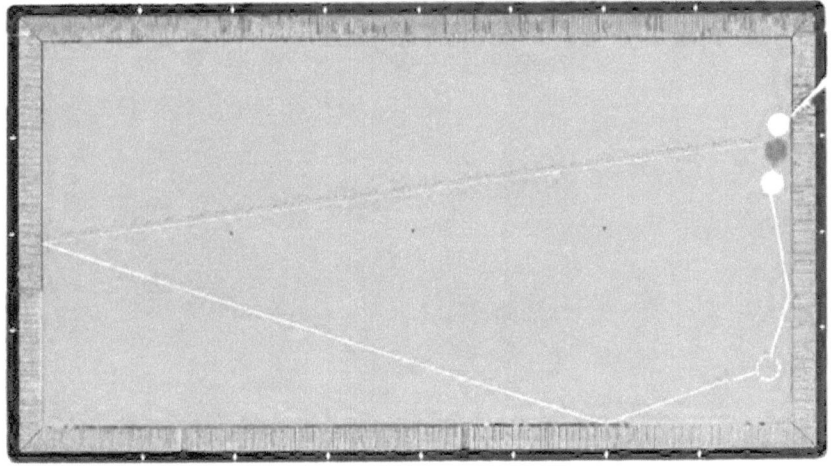

No. 50.—"Kiss-Shot."

Strike your own ball on top and a little to the left, the red ball one-quarter, the cue-ball will go the length of the table to the lower end-cushion and back, meeting the second object-ball as it is driven by the red ball along the upper end-cushion.

GARNIER'S PRACTICE SHOTS. 51

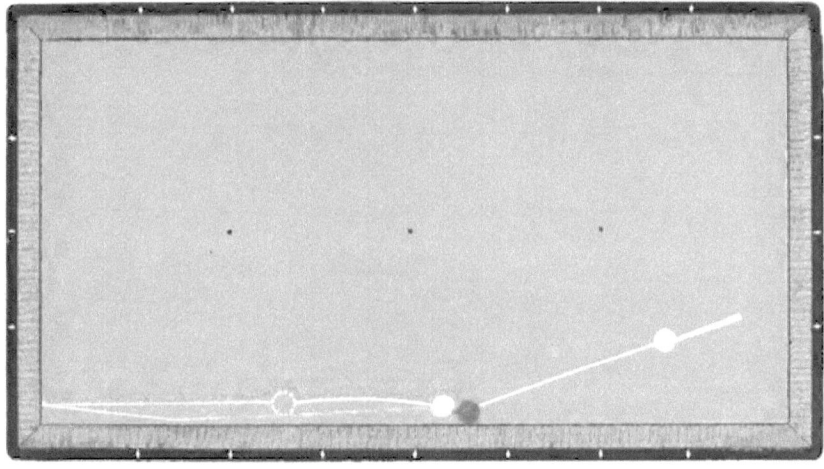

No. 51.—Follow and "Kiss-Shot."

Strike your own ball on top and on the left side, the red ball full, and follow with your own ball along the side-cushion. The red ball will strike the second object-ball full, drive it to the end-cushion, and it will meet the cue-ball as it comes back. This shot should be played with the follow-stroke.

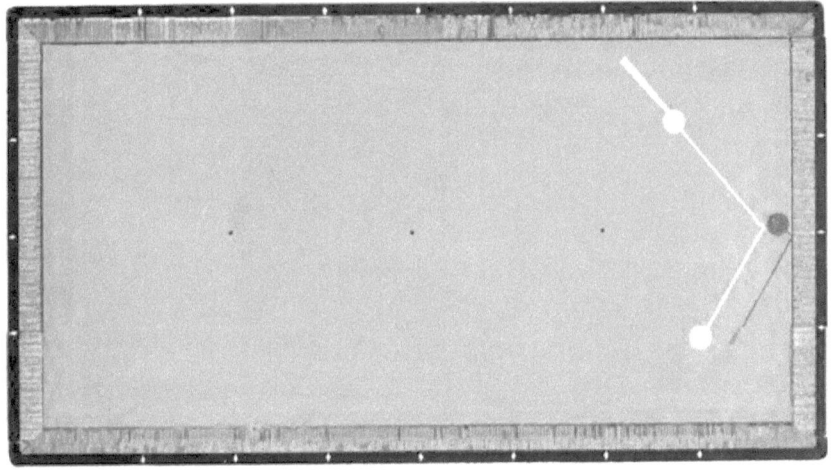

No. 52.—Direct "Kiss-Shot."

Strike your own ball on top and to the left, the red ball about one-third, and the shot will be made directly from the red ball to the second object-ball. This shot should be played very gently, and the balls will be left together.

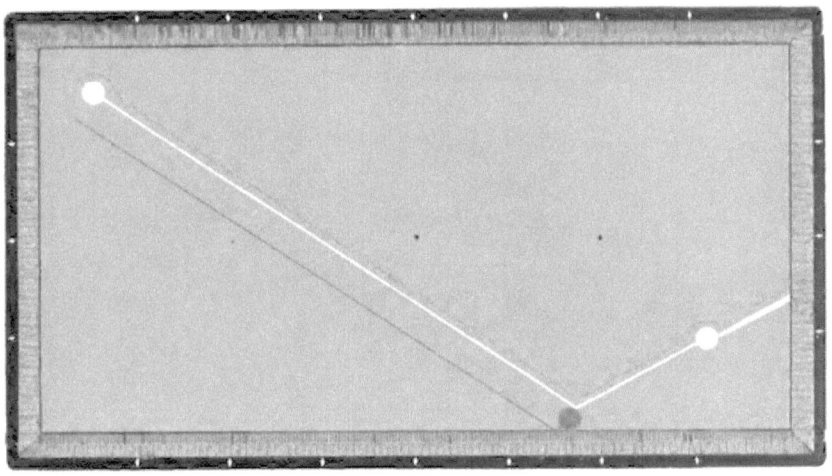

No. 53.—Direct "Kiss" and Gathering-Shot

Strike your own ball on top and on the left side, the red ball almost full, and the shot will be made directly from the red ball to the second object-ball, driving the red ball into the corner with the two white balls, if the shot be not played too "hard." Play this shot with the follow-stroke.

GARNIER'S PRACTICE SHOTS. 54

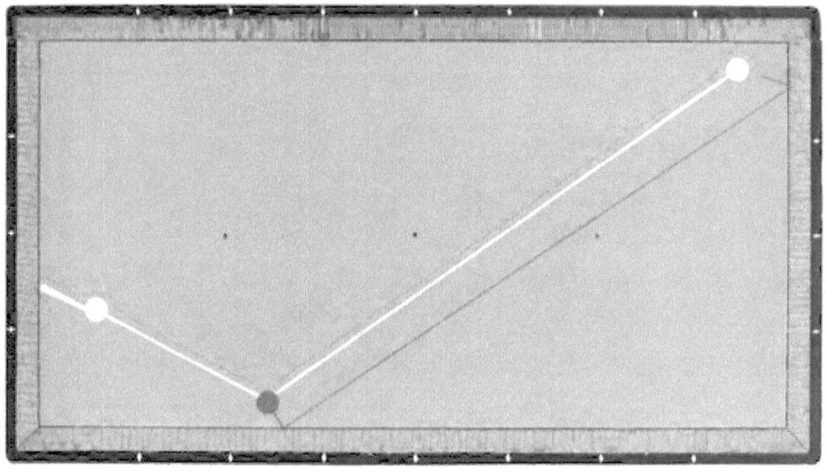

No. 54.—"Kiss" and Gathering-Shot when the Object-Ball does not touch the Cushion.

Strike your own ball on top and on to the right side, the red ball nearly full, and the shot will be made by the kiss. It is necessary to play this shot a little "harder" than the preceding shot, but otherwise the play is the same.

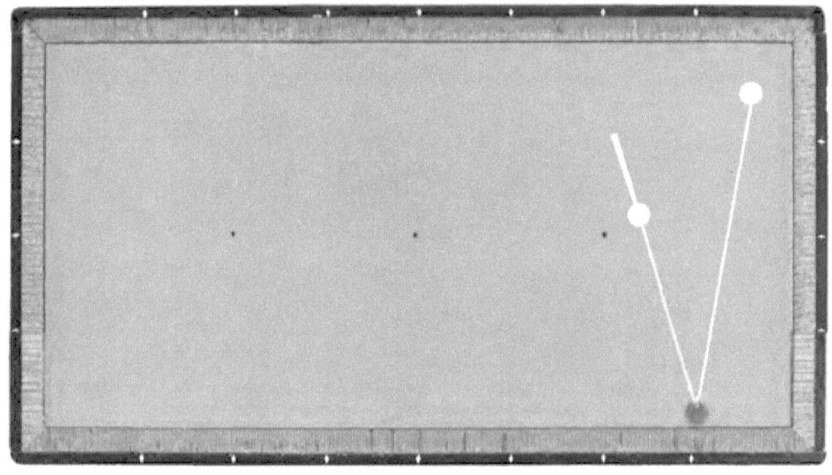

No. 55.—Direct "Kiss-Shot" without Side-Effect.

Strike your own ball very low down and without side-effect, the red ball nearly full, and the shot will be made directly, without a cushion.

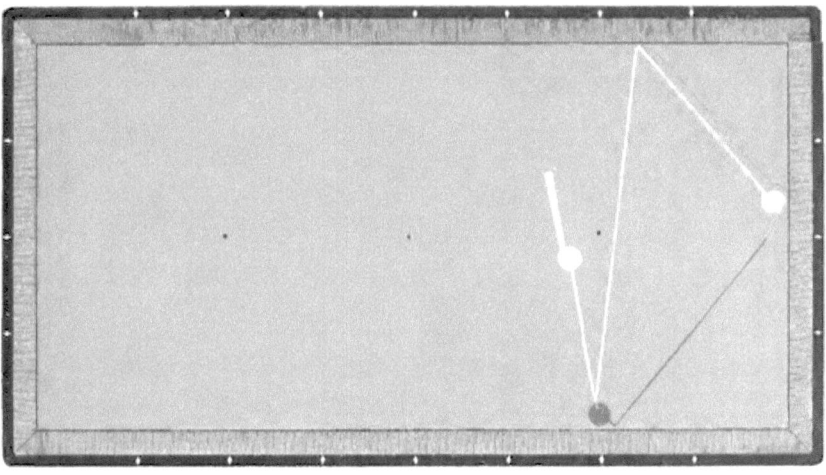

No. 56.—"Kiss" and Cushion-Shot.

Strike your own ball very low down and to the right, the red ball full, the cue-ball will go to the side-cushion, and the side-effect will direct it to the second object-ball, the red ball joining the two white balls near the end-cushion.

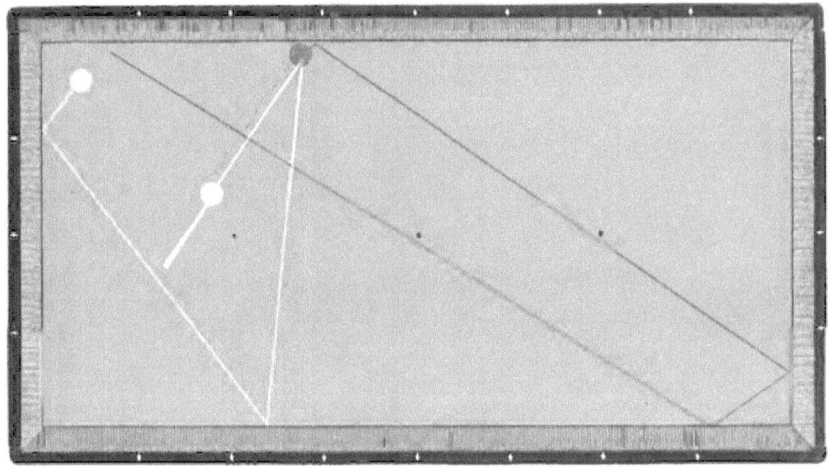

No. 57.—"Kiss-Shot" with Side-Effect.

Strike your own ball very low down and on the right side, the red ball half-full, and the shot will be made by two cushions, driving the red ball around the table to join the two white balls in the corner.

GARNIER'S PRACTICE SHOTS.

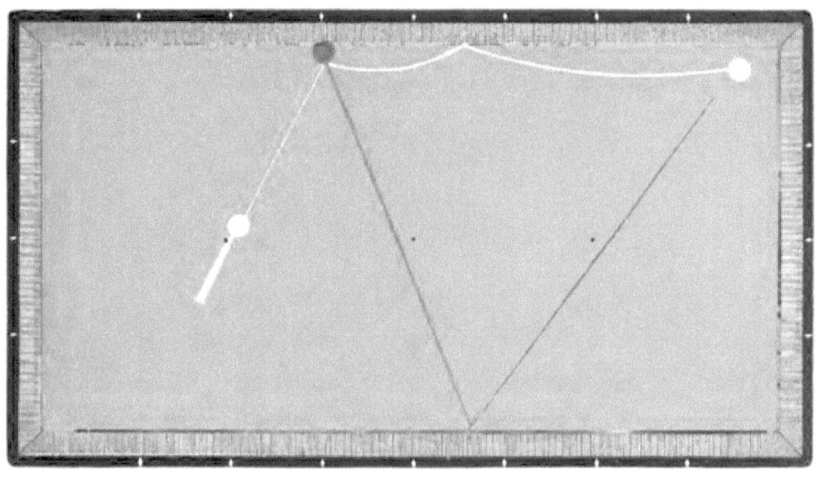

No. 58.—" Kiss-Shot" by the Cushion.

Strike your own ball on top and slightly to the left, the red ball a little less than half-full to the right, and the shot will be made by one cushion. Play this shot with a free stroke.

GARNIER'S PRACTICE SHOTS. 59

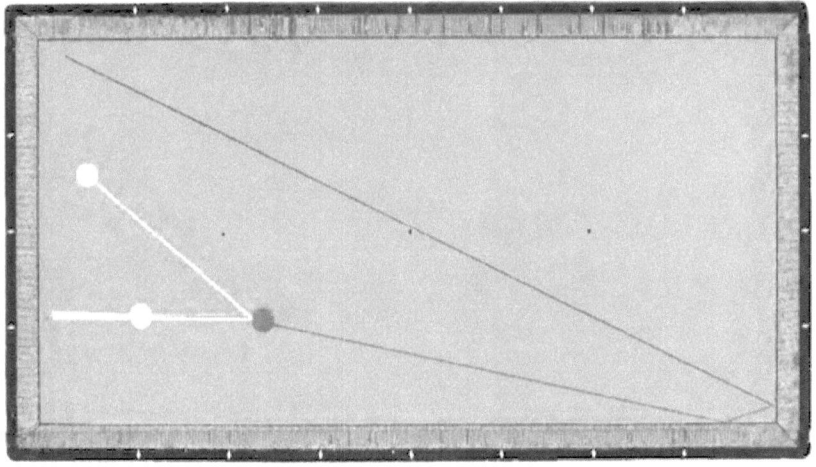

No. 59.—DRAW-SHOT.

Strike your own ball low down, holding the cue very lightly and being particularly careful not to draw the cue back in making the stroke (a very common fault in making draw-shots). Strike the red ball a little to the left, and the shot will be made, driving the red ball the length of the table and into the corner. Use no side-effect. The direction of the draw is determined entirely by the point at which the cue-ball strikes the object-ball.

GARNIER'S PRACTICE SHOTS.   60

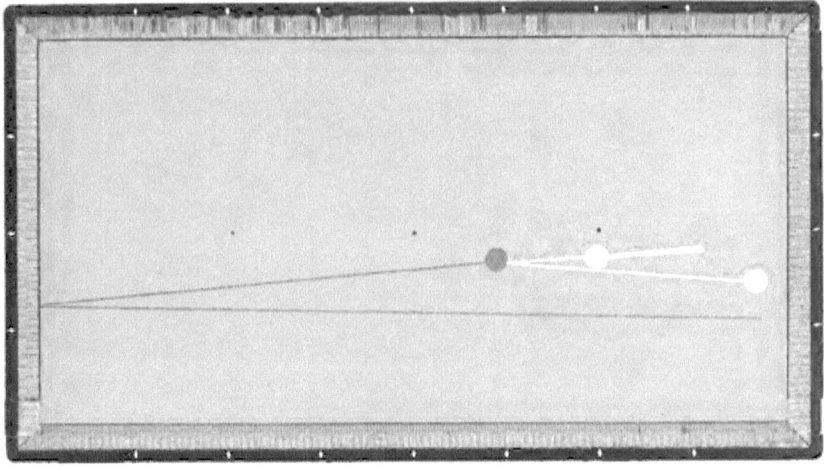

No. 60.—Draw-Shot.

This shot is played in the same way as the preceding shot, except that it is necessary to strike the object-ball fuller. Play the shot with just sufficient force to bring the red ball back to the end-cushion.

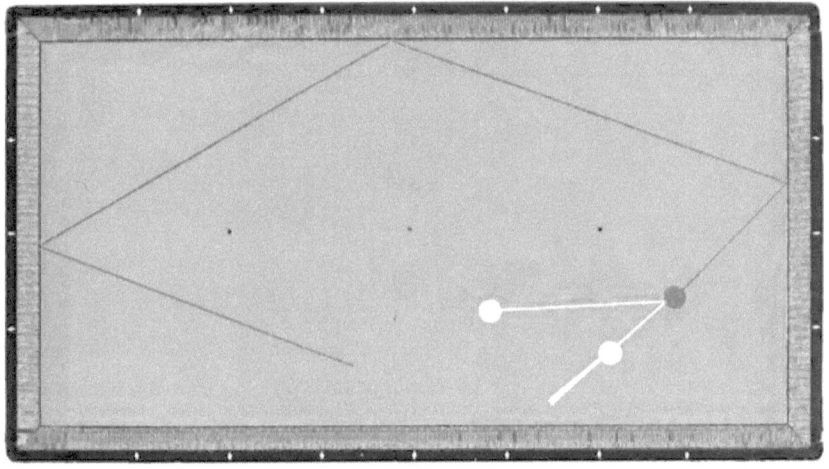

No. 61.—Gathering Draw-Shot.

Draw directly from the red ball to the white ball, without side-effect, and play with sufficient force to drive the red ball around the table to join the two white balls.

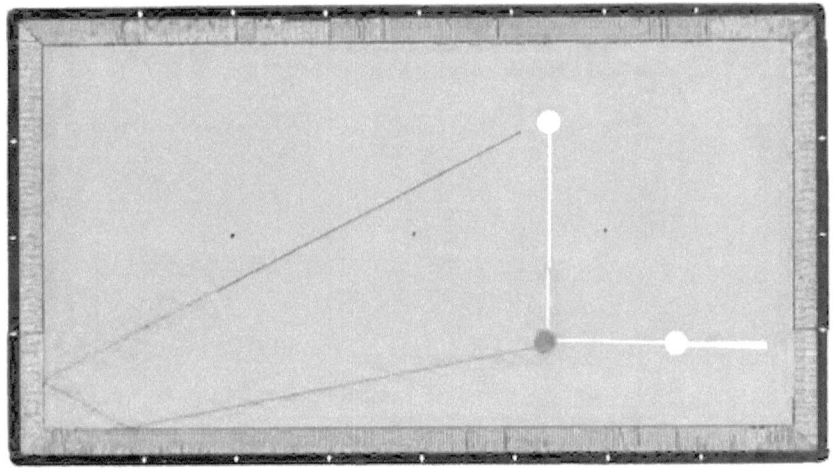

No. 62.—FORCE, OR SPREAD-SHOT.

Strike your own ball low down, the red ball about one-quarter, and the shot will be made directly. Use no side-effect. The direction of the cue-ball depends entirely upon the point where the object-ball is struck. Play with just enough force to bring the red ball back near the other balls.

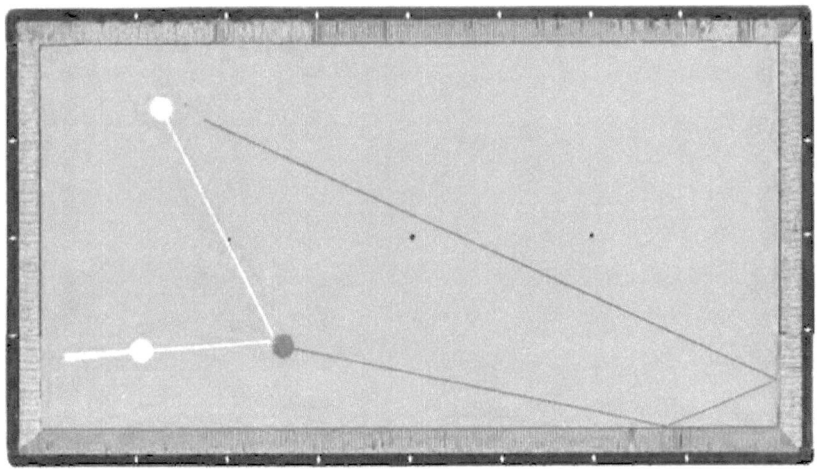

No. 63.—Force-Shot.

Play this shot in the same way as the preceding shot (except that the red ball should be struck about one-third), without side-effect. Endeavor to gather the balls in the corner.

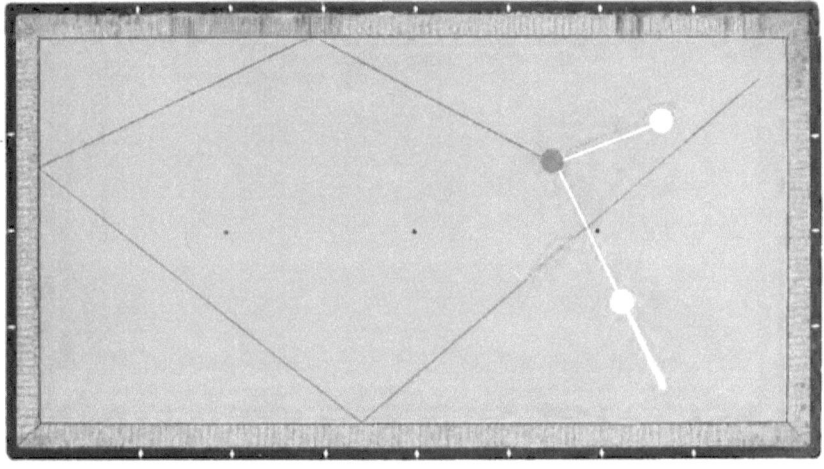

No. 64.—GATHERING FORCE-SHOT.

Strike your own ball low down and the red ball about as indicated in the diagram. The shot will be made directly, and the red ball will be driven around the table to join the other balls in the corner. The cue-ball should not be struck too low, but it should be "slowed" so as not to strike the second object-ball too "hard."

GARNIER'S PRACTICE SHOTS. 65

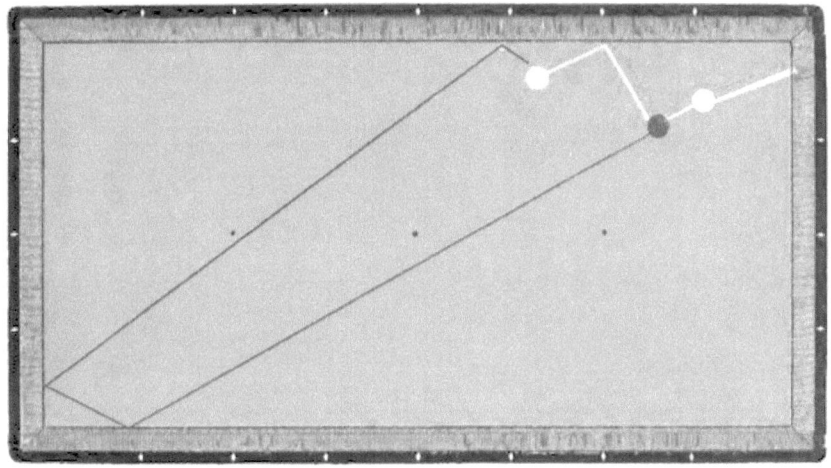

No. 65.—Gathering-Shot

Strike your own ball below the center and on the left side, the red ball nearly full, and the shot will be made by one cushion, leaving the balls together. Hold the cue back slightly in making the stroke.

GARNIER'S PRACTICE SHOTS.

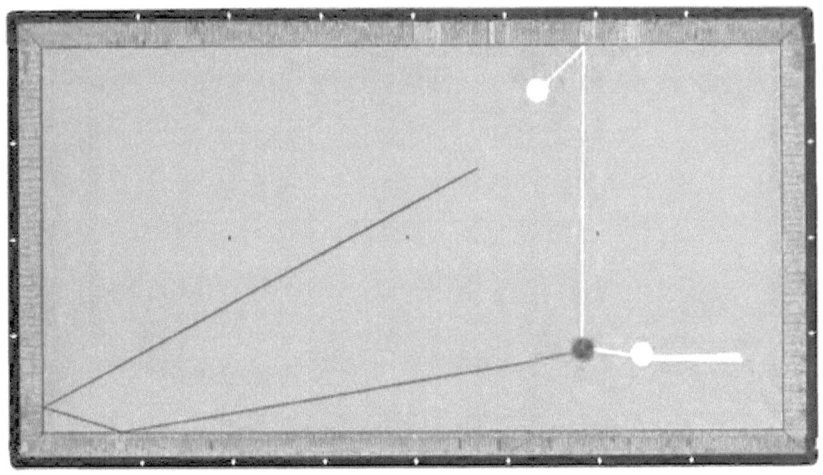

No. 66.—FORCE-SHOT WITH SIDE-EFFECT.

Strike your own ball low down and on the right side, the red ball about one-third, and the shot will be made by the cushion. The object of playing this shot with side-effect, and by the cushion instead of directly, is to bring the balls together.

GARNIER'S PRACTICE SHOTS. 67

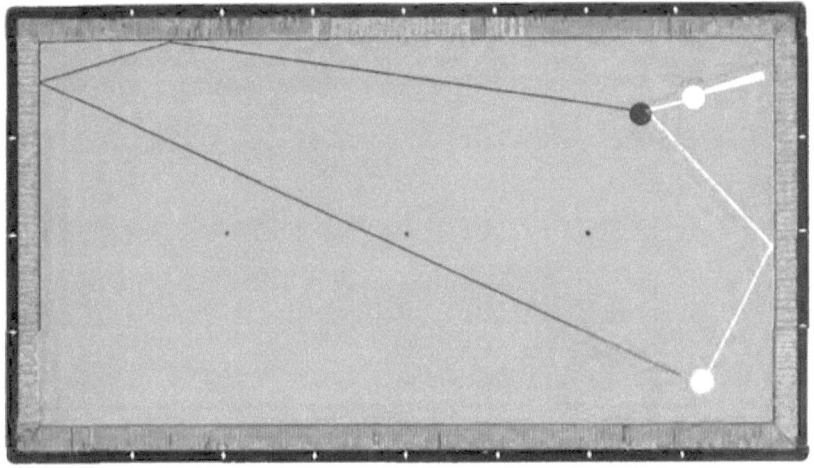

No. 67.—DRAW AND CUSHION-SHOT, WITH REVERSE-EFFECT.

Strike your own ball low down and on the right side, the red ball about one-third, and the shot will be made by one cushion. The object in making the shot by the cushion is to bring the balls together in the corner.

GARNIER'S PRACTICE SHOTS.

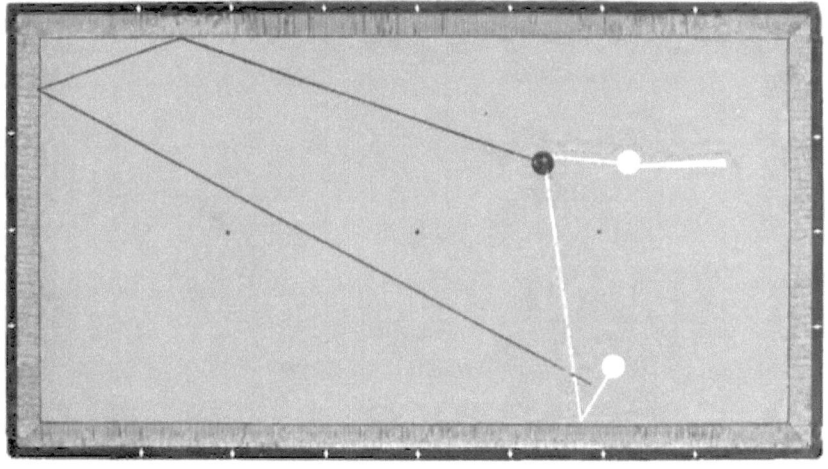

No. 68.—Force and Cushion-Shot.

Strike your own ball low down and on the left side, the red ball one-quarter, and the shot will be made by the side-cushion. The object of the play by the cushion is to bring the balls together.

GARNIER'S PRACTICE SHOTS.

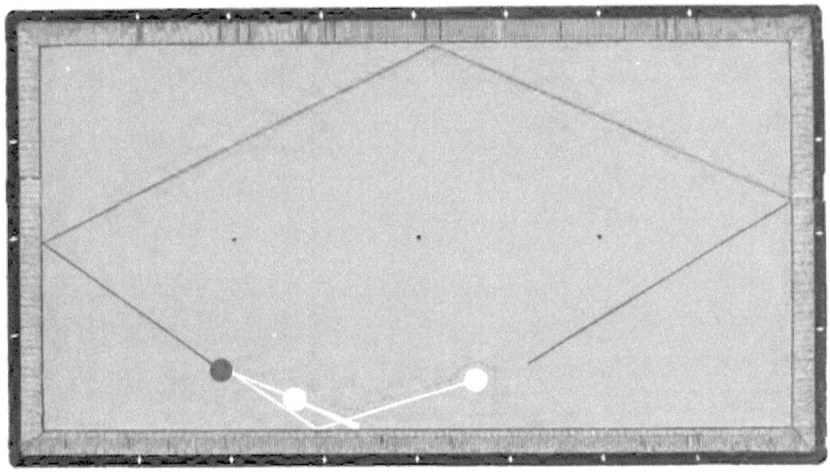

No. 69.—DRAW AND CUSHION-SHOT.

Strike your own ball low down and a little to the left, the red ball nearly full, and the shot will be made by the cushion. In the position of the balls indicated in the diagram, this is the easiest way to leave them together after making the shot.

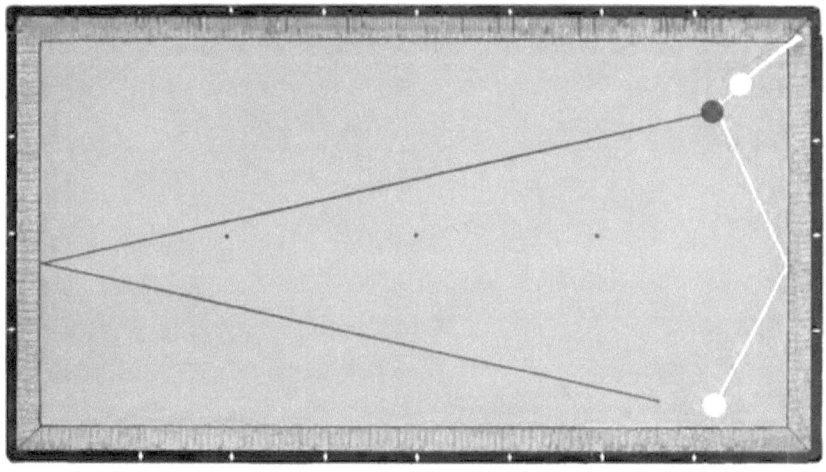

No. 70.—Force and Cushion-Shot.

Strike your own ball a little below the center and on the right side, the red ball about half-full, and the shot will be made by the end-cushion, bringing the balls together in the corner. Play this shot with a sharp, quick stroke.

GARNIER'S PRACTICE SHOTS. 71

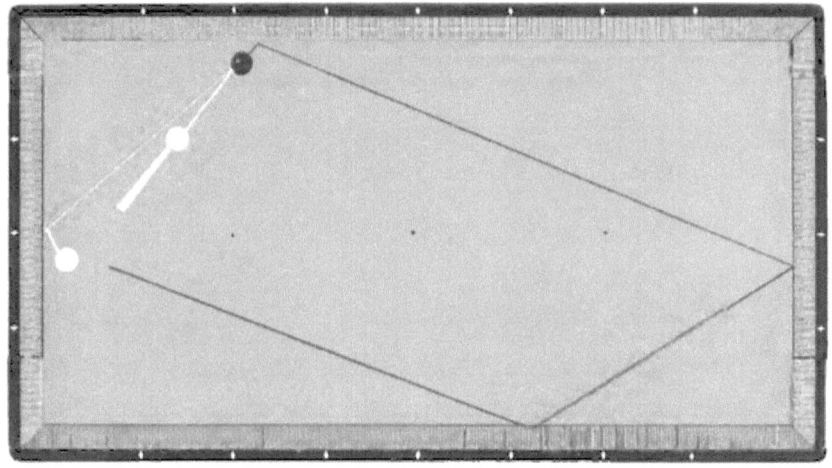

No. 71.—GATHERING DRAW-SHOT.

Draw from the red ball to the white ball by the end-cushion, striking your own ball low down and a little to the left. If the shot be played in this way, the balls can be brought together.

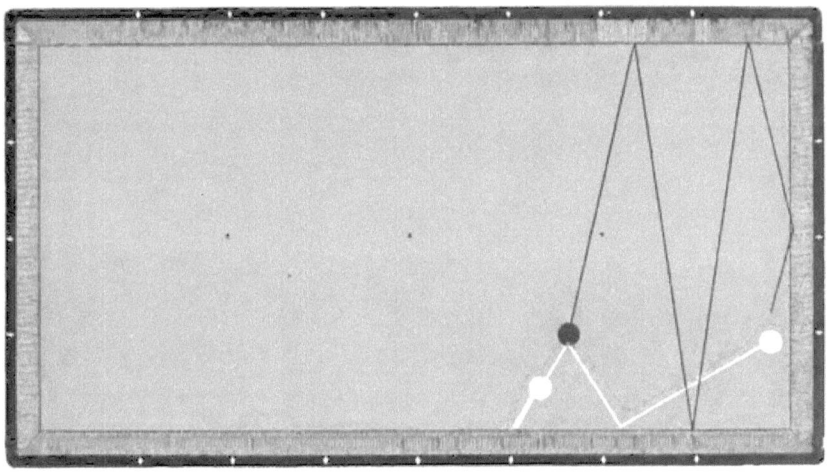

No. 72.—Draw and Cushion-Shot.

Strike your own ball low down and on the left side, the red ball nearly full, and the shot will be made by the cushion. Play this shot "hard," in order to cross the red ball twice.

GARNIER'S PRACTICE SHOTS. 73

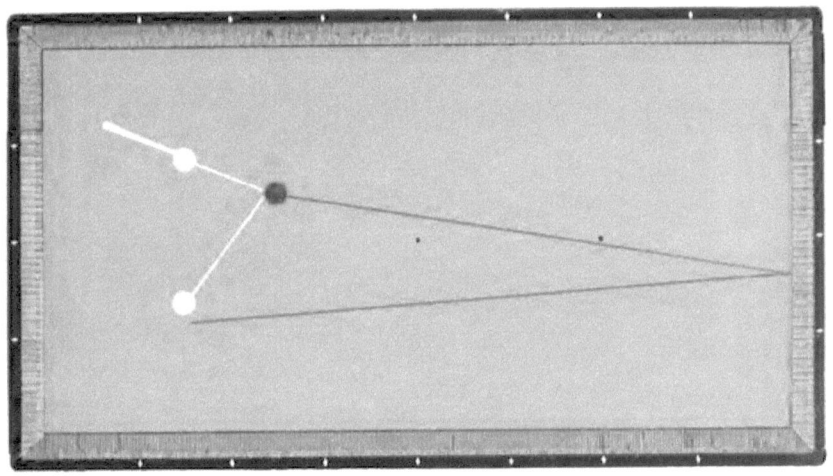

No. 73.—Force-Shot, with Reverse-Effect.

Strike your own ball low down and a little to the left, the red ball half-full, and the shot will be made directly. The object of the reverse-effect is to slow the cue-ball, while the red ball is struck with force enough to bring it back to join the other balls.

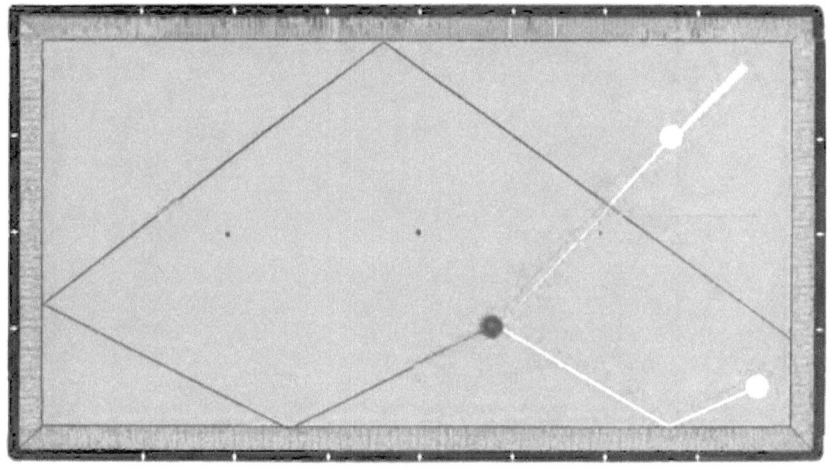

No. 74.—Gathering-Shot.

Strike your own ball rather low down and on the left side, the red ball one-third, and the shot will be made by one cushion. Play the shot moderately "hard" in order to bring the balls together in the corner.

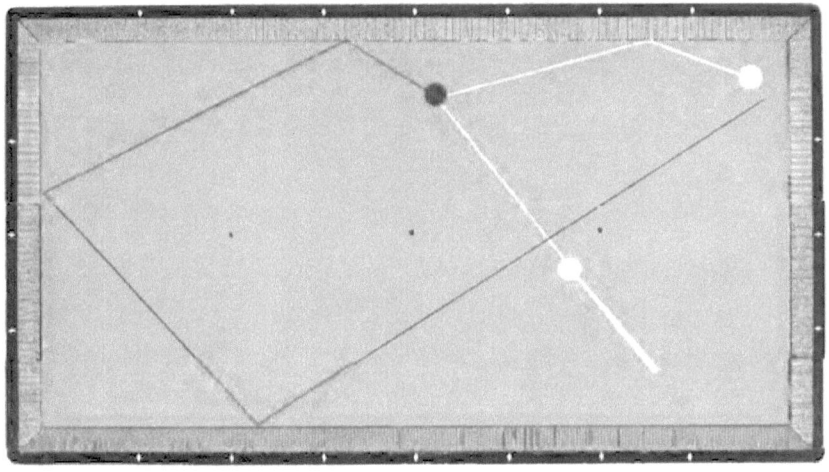

No. 75.—Gathering-Shot.

Strike your own ball low down and on the right side, the red ball half-full, and the shot will be made by one cushion. Play the shot moderately "hard" in order to bring the balls together in the corner.

GARNIER'S PRACTICE SHOTS. 76

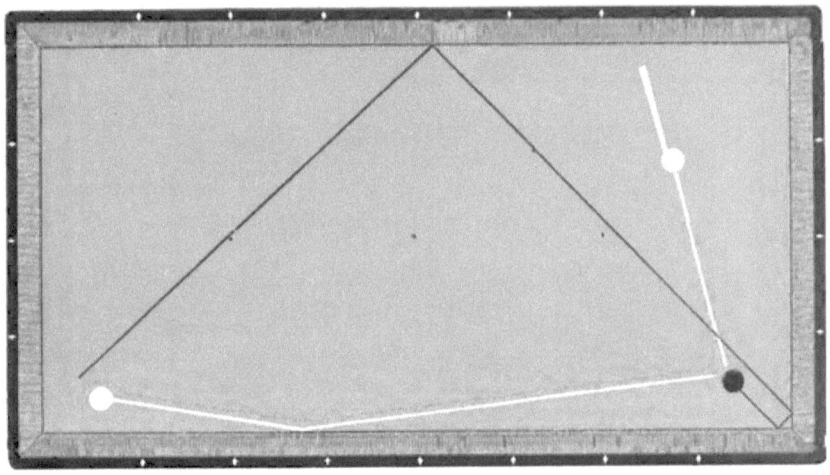

No. 76.—GATHERING-SHOT.

Strike your own ball very low down and on the right side, the red ball half-full, and the shot will be made by one cushion. Play the shot moderately "hard" in order to bring the balls together in the corner.

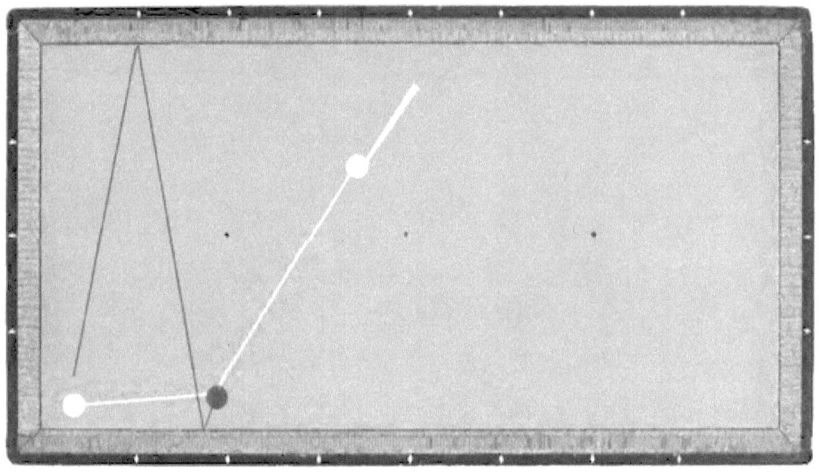

No. 77.—Direct-Shot with Reverse-Effect.

Strike your own ball in the middle and on the left side (which will "slow" the cue-ball), the red ball nearly full and you will make the direct shot, bringing the balls together in the corner. Play the shot moderately "hard."

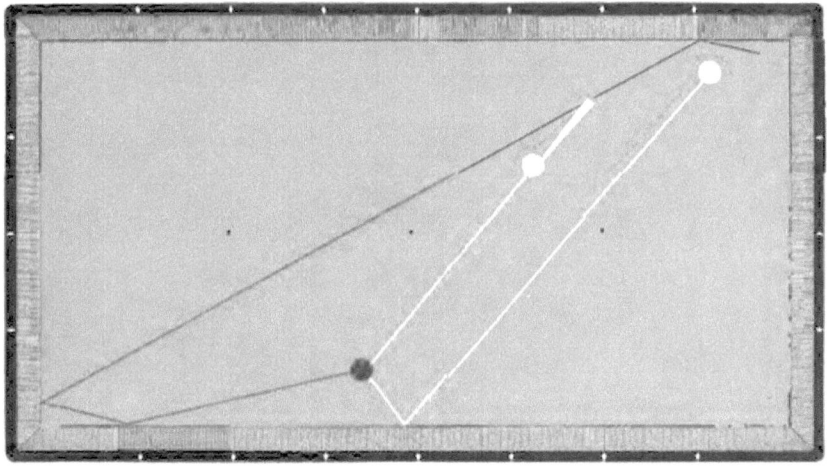

No. 78.—Gathering Shot.

Strike your own ball a little below the center and on the left side, the red ball one-quarter, and the shot will be made by one cushion. Play the shot rather "hard" in order to bring the balls together in the corner.

GARNIER'S PRACTICE SHOTS. 79

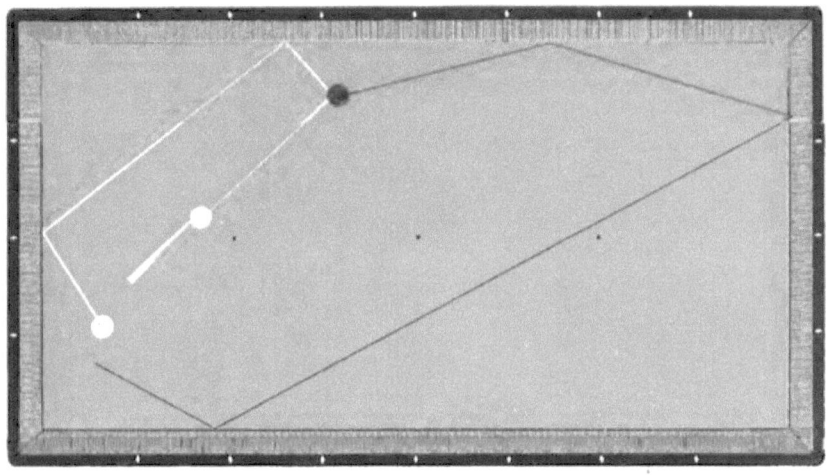

No. 79.—GATHERING-SHOT.

Strike your own ball a little below the center and on the left side, the red ball one-third, and the shot will be made by two cushions. Play the shot rather "hard" in order to bring the balls together.

GARNIER'S PRACTICE SHOTS. 80

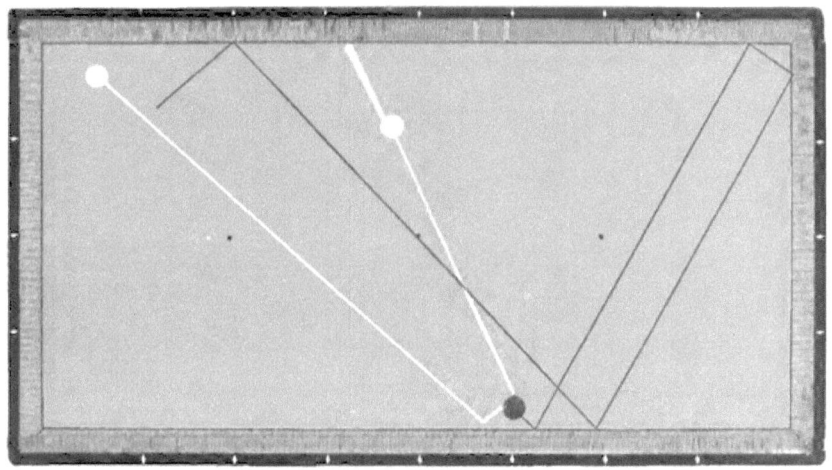

No. 80.—GATHERING-SHOT.

Strike your own ball moderately low down and on the right side, the red ball nearly full, and the shot will be made by one cushion, possibly bringing the balls together near the corner. Play this shot rather "hard."

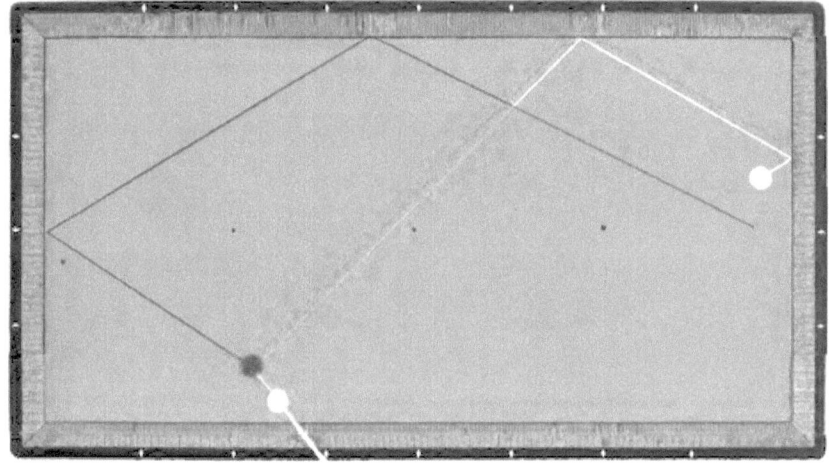

No. 81.—Gathering-Shot.

Strike your own ball about the middle and on the right side, the red ball about one-third, and the shot will be made by one or two cushions, leaving the balls together. This shot should be played with a quick, sharp stroke.

GARNIER'S PRACTICE SHOTS. 82

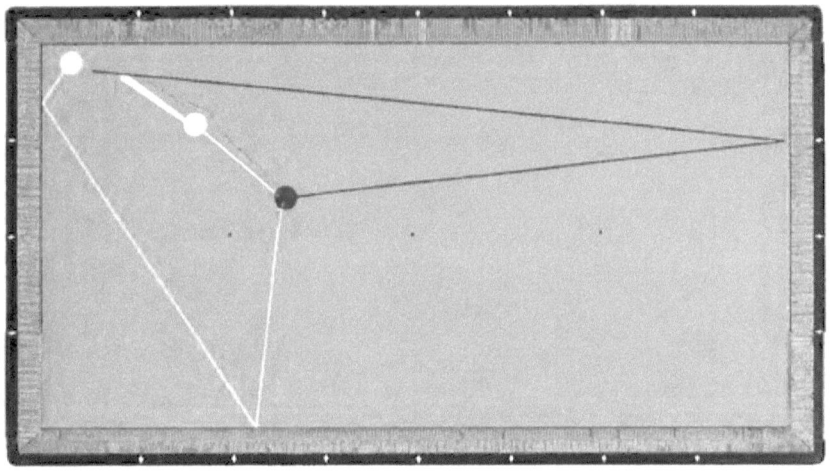

No. 82.—Gathering-Shot.

Strike your own ball low down and on the right side, the red ball one-quarter, and the shot will be made by two cushions, gathering the balls in the corner.

GARNIER'S PRACTICE SHOTS.

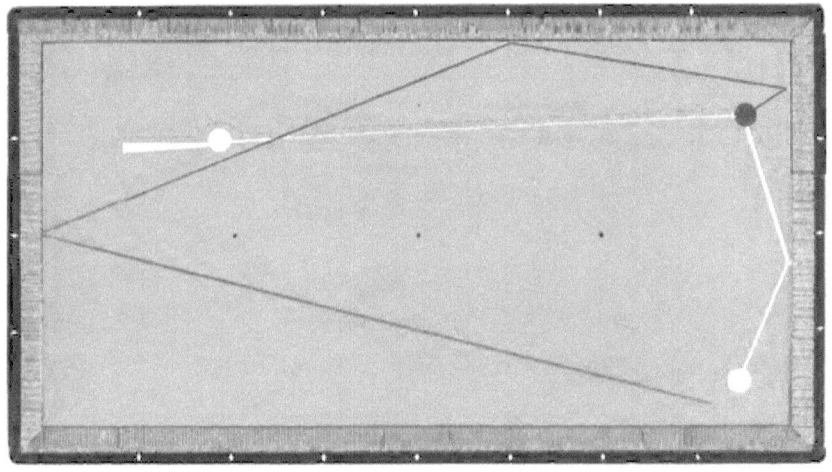

No. 83.—Gathering-Shot.

Strike your own ball rather low down and on the right side, the red ball nearly full and rather "hard," so as to bring the ball into the corner, and the shot will be made by one cushion. The cue-ball should be "slowed" in playing this shot.

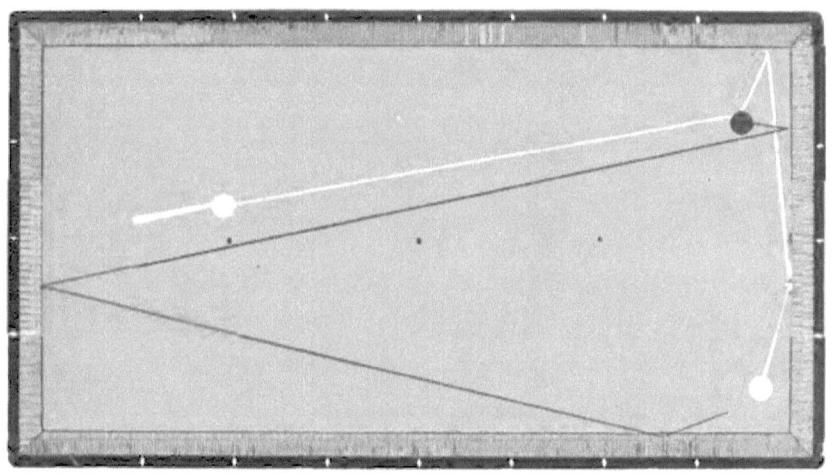

No. 84.—Shot across the Table (Gathering).

Strike your own ball low down and on the left side, the red ball one-quarter, and the shot will be made by two cushions, bringing the balls together in the corner.

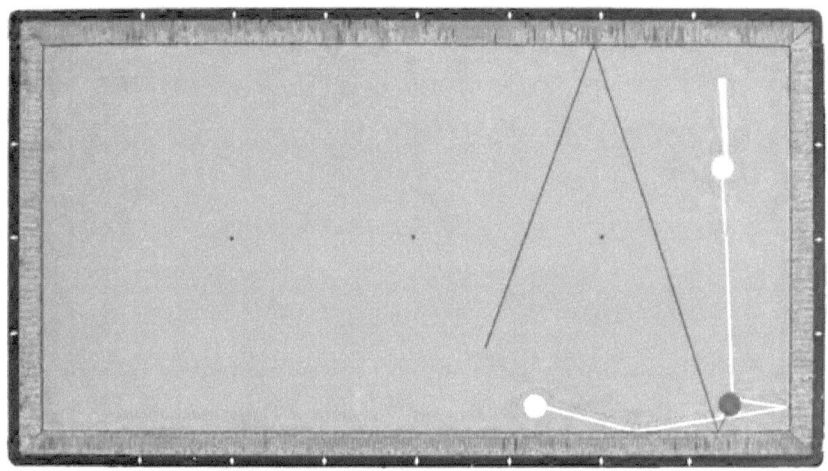

No. 85.—Shot with Reverse-Effect.

Strike your own ball a little below the center and on the right side, the red ball almost full, and the shot will be made by two cushions, crossing the red ball to the side-cushion. The object in playing this shot by the end-cushion is to bring the balls together.

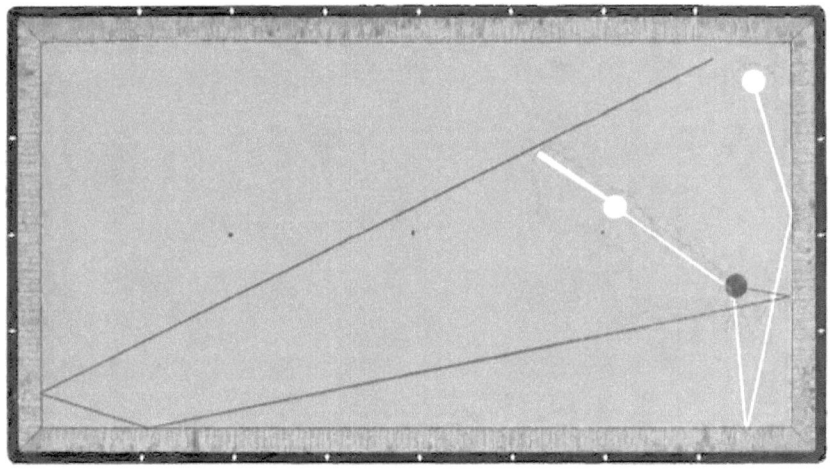

No. 86.—Shot across the Table (Gathering).

Strike your own ball a little below the center and on the left side, the red ball half-full, and the shot will be made by two cushions, bringing the balls together in the corner. The cue-ball is "slowed" in making this shot.

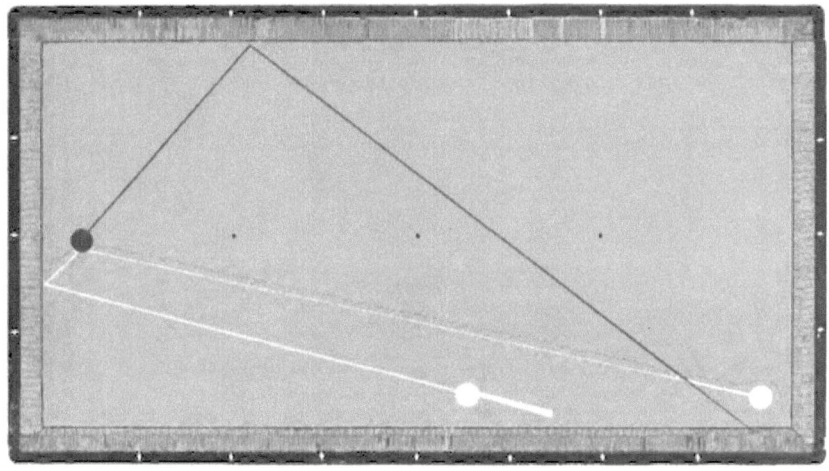

No. 87.—Cushion-first Shot the Length of the Table.

Strike your own ball about the center and on the right side. Take the end-cushion before striking the red ball, and the shot will be easily made. It is proper to play the shot in this way when the red ball is not more than three or four inches from the end-cushion.

GARNIER'S PRACTICE SHOTS.

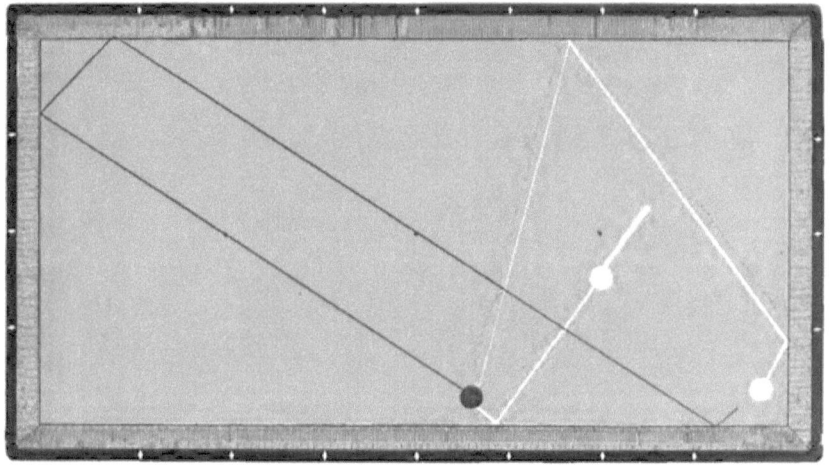

No. 88.—Cushion-first Shot across the Table.

Strike your own ball in the middle and on the right side, the cushion first, and the shot will be made by two cushions after striking the red ball, driving the red ball around the table into the corner. The shot should be played in this way when the object-ball is not more than four or five inches from the cushion.

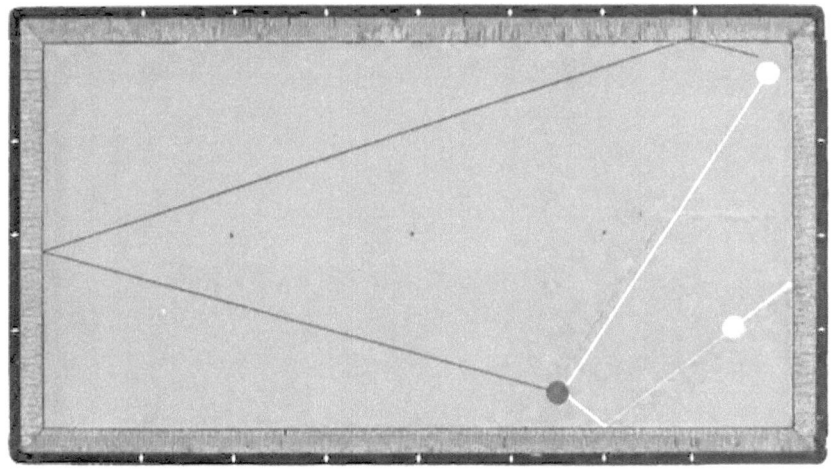

No. 89.—Cushion-first Shot, without Side-Effect.

Strike your own ball low down, without side-effect, the cushion first so as to strike the red ball about one-third, and the shot will be made, bringing the red ball back into the corner to join the two white balls. The shot should be played in this way when the object-ball is from three to four inches from the cushion.

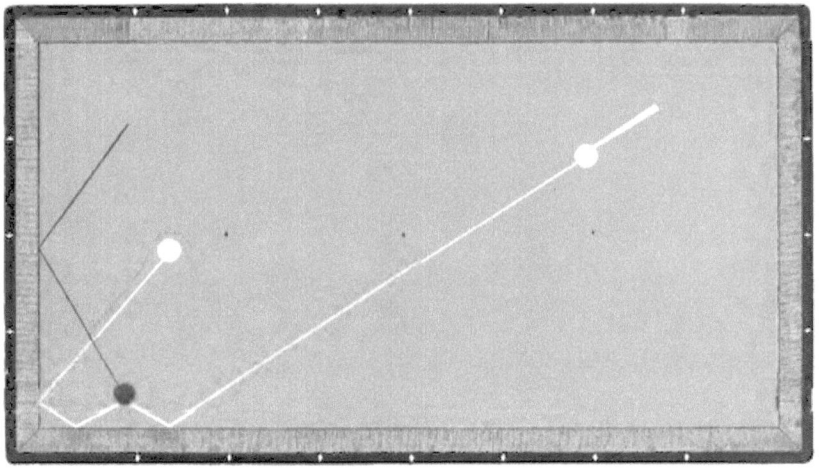

No. 90.—Cushion-first Shot.

Strike your own ball a little below the center and slightly to the right, the cushion first so as to strike the red ball about one-quarter, and the shot will be made by two cushions after striking the red ball, leaving the balls together. This shot should be played rather gently.

GARNIER'S PRACTICE SHOTS.   91

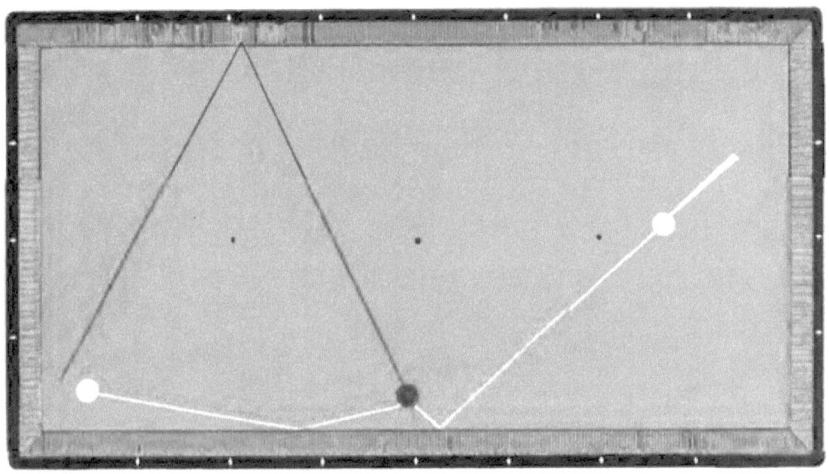

No. 91.—Cushion-first, Gathering-Shot.

Strike your own ball on top and a little to the right, the cushion first, and the shot will be easily made by going behind the ball, bringing the balls together in the corner. The shot played in this way is quite as easy and as certain as the direct shot, and it has the advantage of gathering the balls.

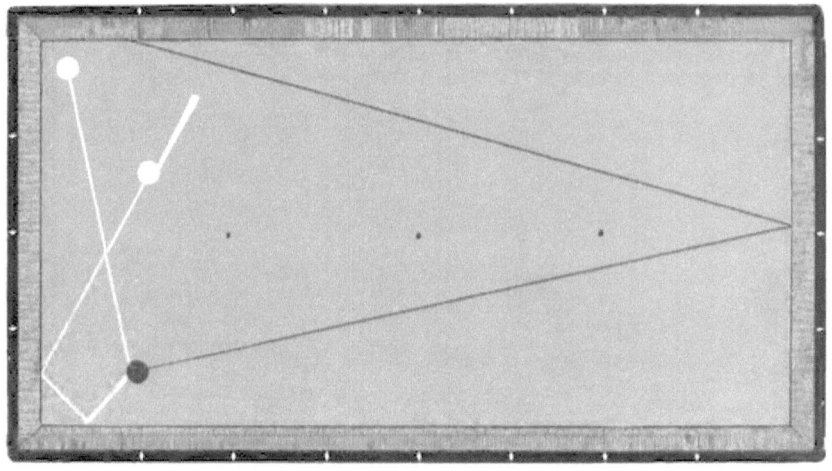

No. 92.—SHOT BY TAKING TWO CUSHIONS FIRST.

Strike your own ball below the center and a little to the left, take two cushions first so as to strike the red ball about one-quarter, and the shot will be easily made, leaving the red ball with the other balls in the corner. Play this shot rather "hard."

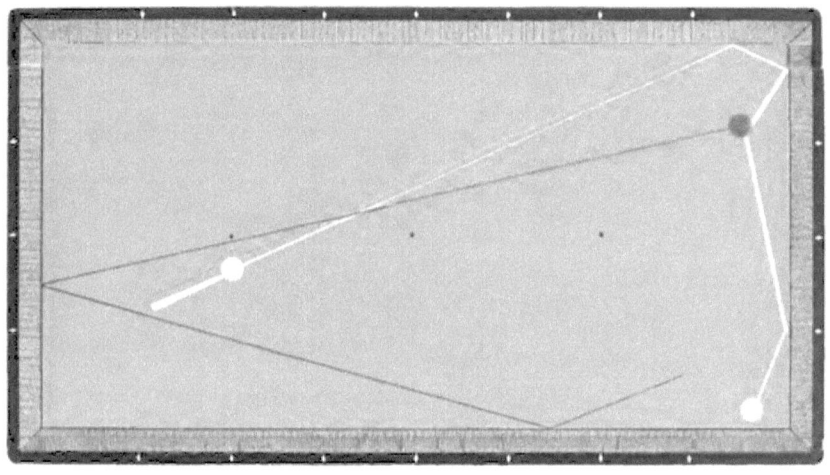

No. 93.—Shot by taking Two Cushions first.

Strike your own ball low down and on the right side, take two cushions first so as to strike the red ball about one-third, and the shot will be made easily by one cushion after striking the red ball. Play this shot rather "hard" in order to bring the red ball back.

GARNIER'S PRACTICE SHOTS. 94

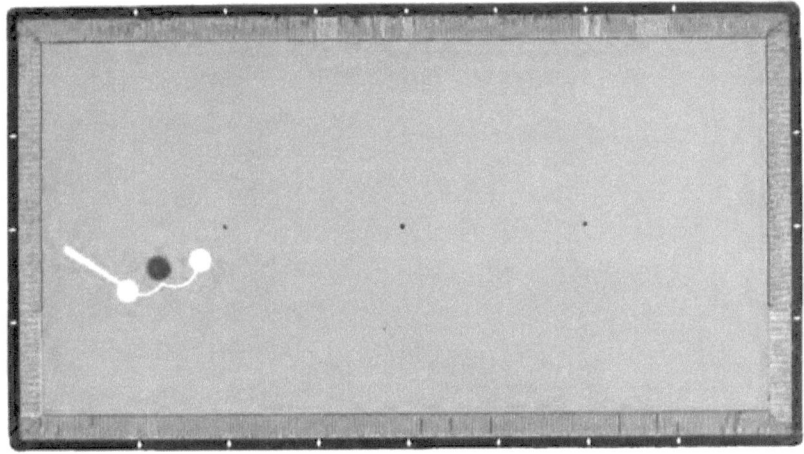

No. 94.—SHORT MASSÉ TO THE RIGHT.

In the *massé*, the cue is held in the right hand with the thumb uppermost, except in the "grand" *massés*, which are seldom played except as "fancy shots." Make a firm bridge on the table with the left hand resting perpendicularly on the middle, third, and little fingers separated from each other as widely as possible. Hold the cue perpendicularly over the ball and lightly between the thumb and the index and middle fingers of the right hand, directing it properly between the thumb and index-finger of the left hand. The but of the cue should pass near the right ear. Strike your own ball perpendicularly one-third and a little to the left, and the shot will be made easily. Strike your ball gently, for the weight of the cue itself dropping upon the ball is nearly sufficient to give the curved direction to the cue-ball. In such shots the cue should always be well chalked.

GARNIER'S PRACTICE SHOTS.

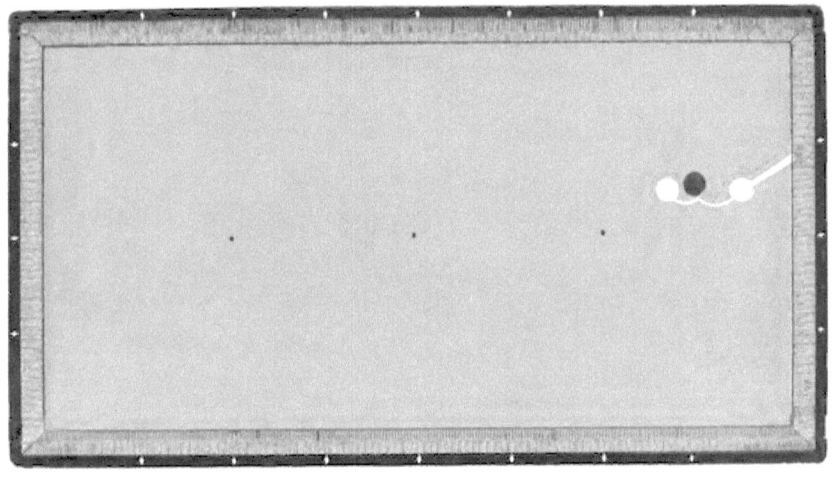

No. 95.—SHORT MASSÉ TO THE LEFT.

Play this shot in the same way as the preceding shot, with the following difference: The but of the cue is removed ten or twelve inches from the head in all *massés* to the left, instead of being near the right ear. The cue-ball is struck perpendicularly and to the right instead of to the left.

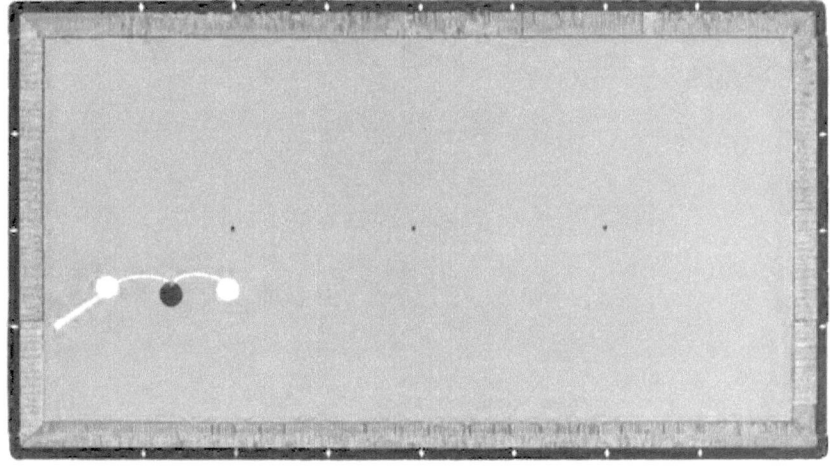

No. 96.—Longer Massé.

This shot is played in the same way as the preceding shot, except that it is made with a little more force.

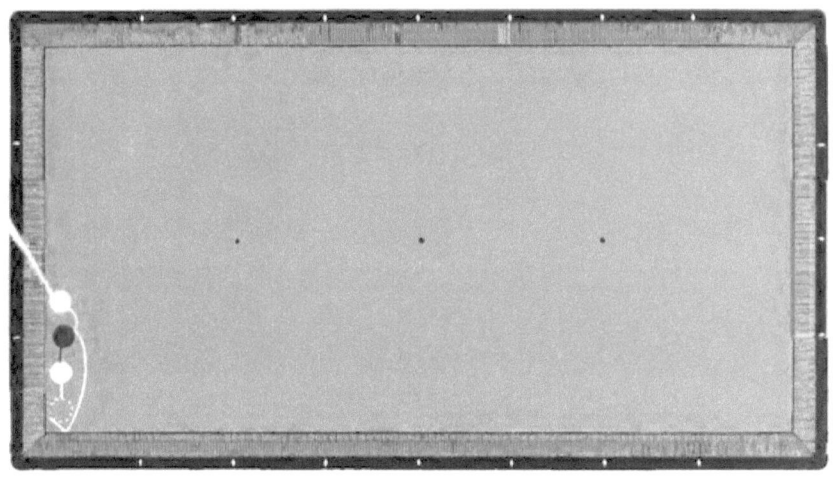

No. 97.—MASSÉ AND "KISS-SHOT."

Play this shot like the preceding, giving your own ball a little more side-effect and playing with a little more force.

GARNIER'S PRACTICE SHOTS. 98

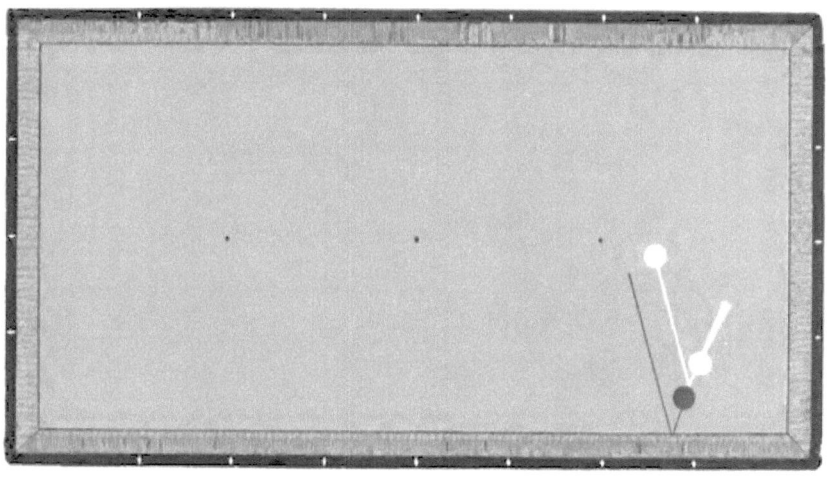

No. 98.—Massé-Draw Shot.

Hold your cue less perpendicularly than in the previously described *massés*, strike your ball near the center and to the right, let the cue drop sharply on the cue-ball, and the shot will be made easily.

GARNIER'S PRACTICE SHOTS.

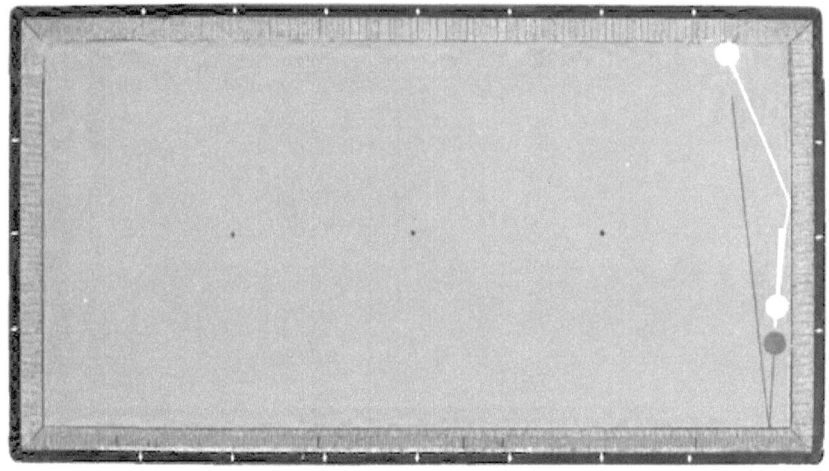

No. 99.—Massé-Draw-and-Cushion Shot.

Strike your own ball as for the short *massé*-draw shot and a little to the left, the red ball full, and the shot will be made by one cushion, driving the red ball across the table to join the two white balls. This shot should be played with more force than the short *massé*-draw shot.

L of C.

GARNIER'S PRACTICE SHOTS. 100

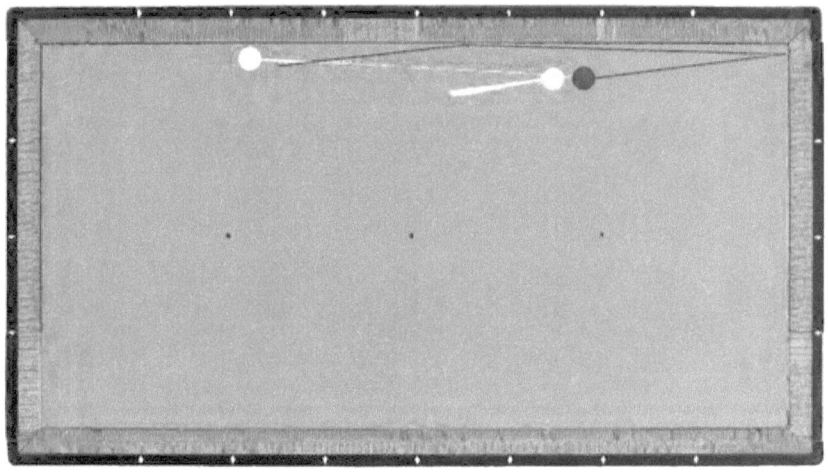

No. 100.—MASSÉ-DRAW SHOT, WITH THE BALLS VERY NEAR TOGETHER.

When the balls are very near each other, there is danger of a push when the bridge is made with the left hand on the table. Play through the thumb and the index-finger of the left hand used as a guide, the left hand being steadied by pressing the elbow firmly against the left side. The left hand is held eight or ten inches above the ball. The cue is held almost perpendicularly and is dropped sharply on the cue-ball a little behind its centre. This shot is not difficult.

GARNIER'S PRACTICE SHOTS. 101

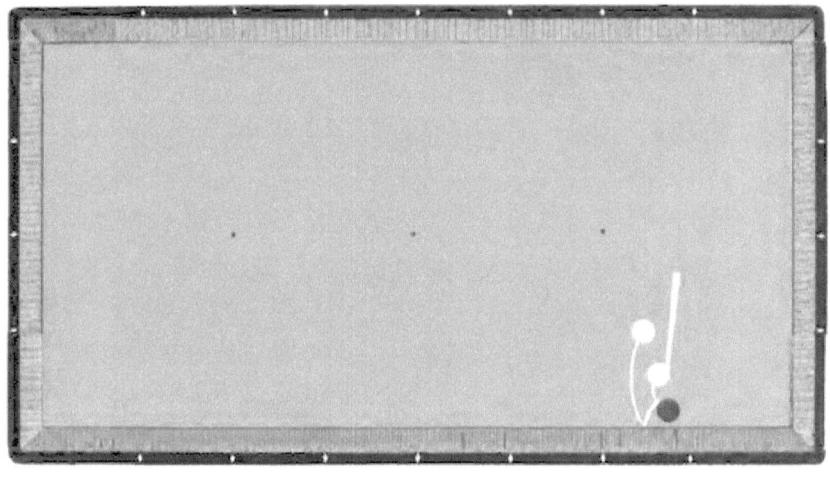

No. 101.—Massé-Cushion Shot.

Strike your own ball, the cue being held perpendicularly as in the other *massés*, rather "hard" and well to the left, and the shot will be made by the cushion. The object of playing the shot in this way is to get a good position for the next shot.

GARNIER'S PRACTICE SHOTS.   102

No. 102.—Massé-Follow-and-Cushion Shot.

When the balls are in line, play a *massé* with a side-effect to the left. The shot will be made by the cushion, and the red ball will be left near the second object-ball.

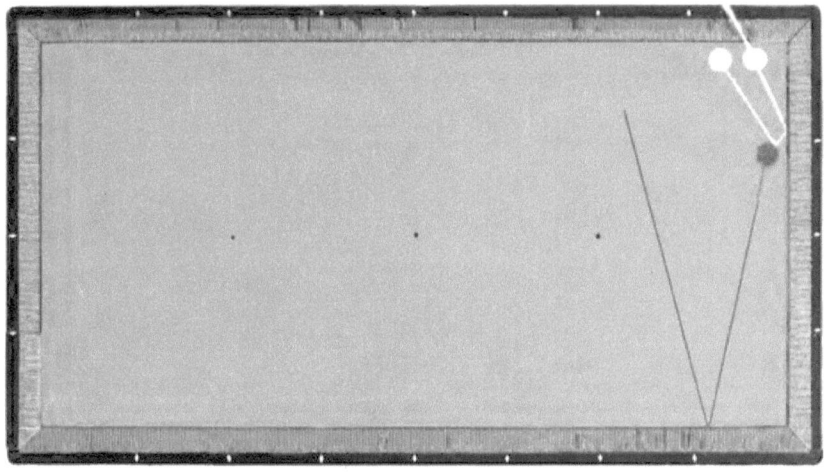

No. 103.—Massé-Draw Shot with the Cushion first.

When your own ball is nearly against the cushion and in the corner, play a *massé*-draw shot, without side-effect, striking the cushion first. This shot should be played rather "hard," and the bridge with the left hand is made on the cushion.

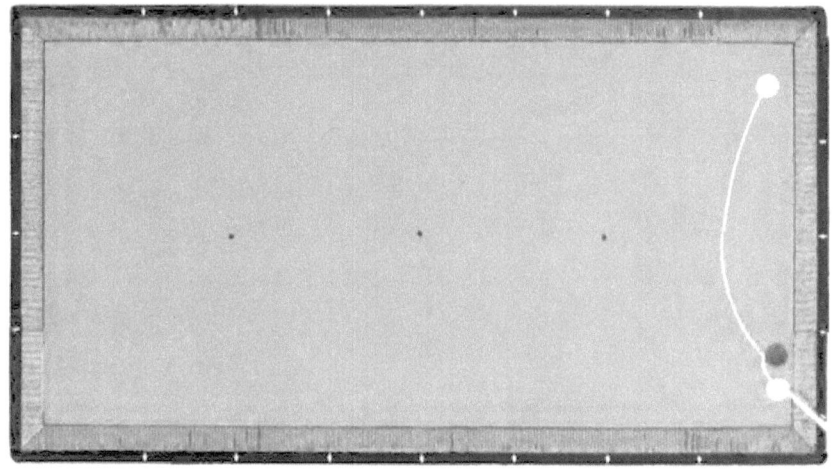

No. 104.—Massé-Shot across the Table.

Raise the cue perpendicularly, make a firm bridge with the left hand, and strike your own ball well to the right with moderate force. The shot is easily made in this way.

GARNIER'S PRACTICE SHOTS.   105

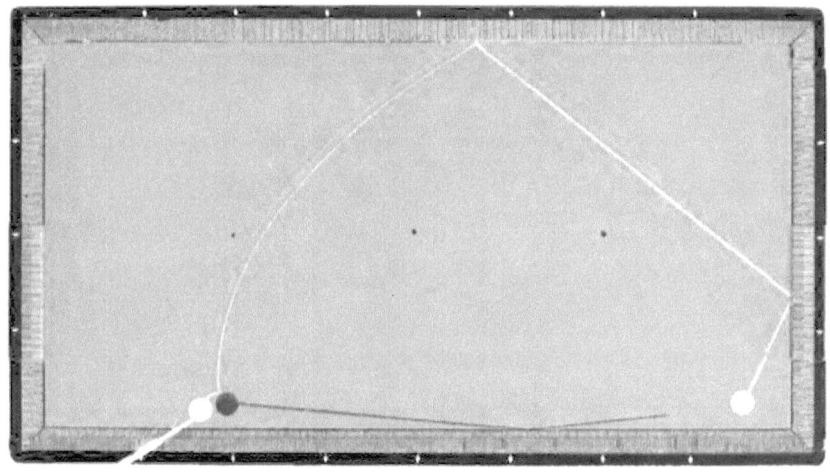

No. 105.—Massé-Shot with Two Cushions.

Make a firm bridge with the left hand, hold the cue perpendicularly, strike your own ball on top and to the right with considerable force, and the shot will be made by two cushions, driving the red ball along the side-cushion to join the two white balls.

GARNIER'S PRACTICE SHOTS. 106

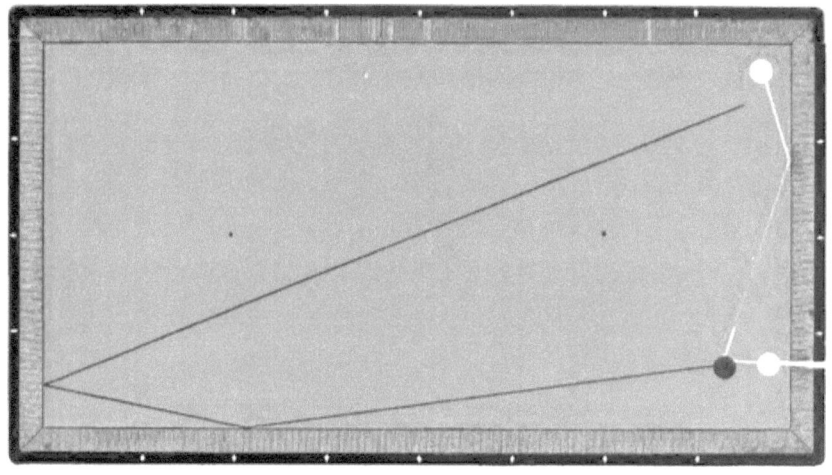

No. 106.—Massé-Draw-and-Cushion Shot.

Play over a firm bridge made with the left hand on the cushion. Hold the cue perpendicularly, strike your own ball on top and a little to the right, and the shot will be made by one cushion. Play with sufficient force to bring the red ball back into the right corner to join the two white balls.

APPENDIX.

RULES OF THE THREE-BALL (FRENCH) GAME,

Adopted by the Contestants in the International Tournament for the Championship of the World, New York, June 23-30, 1873.

THE three-ball carrom game is (as the name indicates) played with three balls, two white and one red. The billiard-table has three spots in a line, dividing the table lengthwise, running from the center of the head-cushion to the center of the foot-cushion; one of those spots, cutting the line in two equal parts, is called the center spot, and the other two are situated half-way between the center spot and the head and foot cushions.

The spot at the head of the table is called the white spot, and the one at the foot of the table, the red spot. The center spot is only used when a ball forced off the table finds both white and red spots occupied. Therefore, should the white ball forced off the table have its spot occupied, it would be placed on the red spot, or on the white spot if it be the red ball that is forced off the table.

APPENDIX.

In beginning the game the red ball and one white are placed on their respective spots; the other white remains in hand, and is placed near the white spot previous to the opening stroke in the game. The player can take any position within six inches of the white spot, on a line parallel or nearly parallel with the head-cushion, but he must strike the red ball first before a count can be effected.

In playing the game the following rules should be observed:

RULES.

1. The game is begun by stringing for the lead; the player who brings his ball nearest to the cushion at the head of the table winning the choice of balls and the right to play first, as in the American game. Should the player fail to count, his opponent then makes the next play, aiming at will at either ball on the table.

2. A carrom consists in hitting both object-balls with the cue-ball, in a fair and unobjectionable way; each will count one for the player. A penalty of one shall also be counted against the player for every miss occurring during the game.

3. A ball forced off the table is put back on its proper spot. Should the player's ball jump off the table after counting, the count is good, the ball is spotted, and the player plays from the spot.

4. If in playing a shot the cue is not withdrawn from the cue-ball before the cue-ball comes in contact with the object-ball, the shot is foul, the player loses his count, and his hand is out.

5. If the balls are disturbed accidentally through the medium of any agency other than the player himself, they must be replaced and the player allowed to proceed.

6. If, in the act of playing, the player disturbs any ball other than his own, he can not make a counting stroke, but he may play for safety. Should he disturb a ball after having played successfully, he loses his count on that shot; his hand is out, and the ball so disturbed is placed back as near as possible in the position which it formerly occupied on the table, the other balls remaining where they stop.

7. Should a player touch his own ball with the cue or otherwise previous to playing, it is foul; the player loses one, and can not play for safety. It sometimes happens that the player, after having

touched his ball, gives a second stroke; then the balls remain where they stop or are replaced as near as possible in their former position at the option of his opponent.

8. When the cue-ball is very near another, the player shall not play without warning his adversary that they do not touch and giving him sufficient time to satisfy himself on that point.

9. When the cue-ball is in contact with another, the balls are spotted, and the player plays with his ball in hand.

10. Playing with the wrong ball is foul. However, should the player using the wrong ball play more than one shot with it, he shall be entitled to his score just the same as if he had played with his own; as soon as his hand is out, the white balls must change places, and the game proceed as usual.

11. In all the games for the Challenge Cup, the crotch is debarred. The object-balls shall be considered crotched whenever the centers of both lie within a 4½-inch square at either corner of the table. When the object-balls are so within said square, three counts only will be allowed, except one of the object-balls or both be forced out of it. In case of failure by the player, his hand is out, and the next player goes on to play with the balls in position as left by the last player.

12. In this game no player is allowed to withdraw before the game is out; by so doing, he forfeits the game. The decision of the referee is final, but it might happen, under extraordinary circumstances, that one of the players should believe his rights to have been violated by the referee. In such a case he must declare the subject of his grievance and announce that he is playing the game out under protest. Then, should he lose the game, the subject of the grievance is left to the decision of experts mutually agreed upon.

Approved by the Committee:

FRANCOIS UBASSY, MAURICE DALY, JOSEPH DION,
ALBERT GARNIER, CYRILLE DION, JOHN DEERY.

H. W. COLLENDER, *President.*

I. GAYRAUD, *Secretary.*

NEW YORK, *June* 18, 1873.

www.ingramcontent.com/pod-product-compliance
Lightning Source LLC
Chambersburg PA
CBHW021825230426

43669CB00008B/868